THE JEWISH LIGHTS BOOK OF
Fun CLASSROOM
ACTIVITIES

Simple and Seasonal Projects
for Teachers and Students

by Danielle Dardashti and Roni Sarig

Illustrations by Avi Katz

D1516754

JEWISH LIGHTS Publishing
Woodstock, Vermont

The Jewish Lights Book of Fun Classroom Activities:
Simple and Seasonal Projects for Teachers and Students

2004 First Printing
© 2004 by Danielle Dardashti and Roni Sarig
Illustrations © 2004 and 2002 by Jewish Lights Publishing

For information regarding permission to reprint material from this book, please mail or fax your request in writing to Jewish Lights Publishing, Permissions Department, at the address / fax number listed below, or e-mail your request to permissions@jewishlights.com.

Library of Congress Cataloging-in-Publication Data

Available upon request.

ISBN 1-58023-206-X (pbk.)

10   9   8   7   6   5   4   3   2   1

Manufactured in Canada

Cover Design: Tim Holtz

Published by Jewish Lights Publishing
A Division of LongHill Partners, Inc.
Sunset Farm Offices, Route 4, P.O. Box 237
Woodstock, VT 05091
Tel: (802) 457-4000   Fax: (802) 457-4004
www.jewishlights.com

A book for
Uri and Raquel

Contents

Acknowledgments xi
Introduction xv

Part I Holiday Fun

1 Shabbat   3

Can-Do Candlesticks 4
"Kid-ish" Kiddush Cup 5
Danielle's Dough-licious Shabbat Mini-Challah 6
The "Super-Appealing, Spill-Concealing" Tablecloth 8
Making Your Own *Besamim* Box 10
Some Easy-to-Grow Herbs for Your *Besamim* Box 10

2 Rosh Hashanah & Yom Kippur   13

Tooting Your Own Shofar 14
Tashlich: Tossing Your Cookies for the New Year 15
Inside-Out Candied Apple 16
Old Country Nut 'n' Honey Treats 17
A Rosh Hashanah Seder 18
Sending the Very Best New Year's Cards 20
History in the Making: Designing Your Own
    Jewish Calendar 21

3 Sukkot   25

Sukkah-Building Basics 26
Tips for the *Sukkah* "Interior Decorator" 26
Sukkah-in-a-*Sukkah* Centerpiece 27
The Real-Deal *Lulav* Shake 29
The Wacky 'n' Tasty *Lulav* "Shake" 30

4 Simchat Torah   31

Tiny Totin' Torah Scrolls 32
Fun Flags for the Simchah Strut 33

5 Hanukkah   35

Miraculous Menorah Making 36
Dreidel-Playing Basics: How to Be a Gelt-Shark 38
Lip-Licking Latkes 39
Appetizing Applesauce 40
Fry 'em and Try 'em: *Soofganiyot* 41

6 Tu B'Shvat   45

The "Nature Nosh" Tu B'Shvat Seder 46
Classroom Gardening 48
Turning Paper Back into a Tree 50

7 Purim   53

The "Shake-Rattle-and-Roll" *Grogger* 54
"Purim Punim" Face Paints 55
Crowns Fit for a King or Queen 55
Three Points: A Haman Hat Trick 57
What a "Cast" of Characters: Papier-Mâché Puppets 58
The "So-Good-You'll-Eat-Your-Hat" Hamantaschen 59

8 Passover   63

Operation Feather-and-Candle 63
Undercover Matzah 64

A Traditional Ashkenazi *Charoset* 66
Farid's Persian Version *Charoset* 66
Charting the Seder Course 68

9 Yom Ha'Atzmaut (with Yom Ha'Shoah and Yom Ha'Zikaron) 73

The "Stuff-It-'Til-It-Stuffs-You" Falafel 74
Aliza's Spreadable Edible Incredible Hummus 76
Slice 'n' Dice Israeli Salad 77
"Jew"elry 78

10 Lag B'Omer 79

Don't Lag B'hind 80

11 Shavuot 83

Midnight Read and Feed 84
The Land of Cheese Blintzes 84
Prize-Winning Paper Cutting 86

12 Tu B'Av 89

It Takes Tu B'Av to Tango 90
To My Love on Tu B'Av 90

13 Celebrating Secular Holidays in a Jewish Way 93

Part II   Classroom Fun for Anytime

14 Volunteerism: *Mitzvot* & *Tzedakah* 101

Make Your Own *Tzedakah* Box 102
Mitzvot in the Community 104

15 Arts & Crafts—and Fun Things to Eat   109

Mezuzah Magic 109
Cosmic Judaica: Glow-in-the-Dark Stars of David 111
Playful Place Mats 112
How to Grow a Family Tree 113
Shawl-om 115
All-Purpose Candy Clay 117
"Me-shugga" Cookies 119
That's a Wrap! 120
And the Envelopes, Please … 121

16 Sports, Games & Outdoor Fun   123

Like a Maccabi 123
Jewish Scouting for Everyone 124
Go "Ga-Ga" for Ga-Ga 125
Shesh-besh 126
"This Challah's-for-the-Birds" Feeder 126

17 Jewish Music & Dance   129

The Classroom-Friendly Jewish Music Guide 129
Israeli Folk Dancing: *Motza'ei-Shabbat* Fever! 146

18 Jewish Books & Stories for Class   151

Books Fun Guide 151
Make Your Own Books 170

19 Jewish Films & Videos for Class   173

Videos and DVDs Fun Guide 173
Film Fun Guide 179
Making Your Own Jewish Videos 181

20 Internet & Software for Jewish Classrooms   183

Jewish Fun Webguide 183
Surfing the Hebrew-net: Hebrew Fonts on Your Computer 187
Super Software 189

Afterword 196
Appendix of Prayers 197
Appendix of Stencils 208
Index 210

Acknowledgments

This book would not exist if it weren't for our families. To our parents, grandparents, siblings, and extended family: We love all of you deeply and thank you for all that you've given us throughout our lives. And to our kids, who each day help us find new ways to have fun being Jewish.

Many of our family members were directly involved with various aspects of this project: Danielle's father, Hazzan Farid Dardashti, whose patient guidance, vast knowledge, interesting ideas—even his photography skills and recipes—added so much to this book. Sheila Dardashti, Aliza and Michael Friedman, Danny Sarig, Galeet Dardashti, Michelle Dardashti, Hazzan Hamid Dardashti, Yadid Dardashti, and Schelly Dardashti all made specific contributions.

Thanks to the outstanding team at Jewish Lights—Stuart Matlins, Jon Sweeney, Emily Wichland, Sarah McBride, and everyone else who helped put this together. Also to our agents, Sheree Bykofsky and Janet Rosen.

There have been countless other individuals who have played a part in the research and development of this book. We thank each and every one of them for the part they played in helping this project come together. Here are just some of them: Rabbi E. Noach Shapiro; Rabbi Avi Friedman; Rabbi Andy Vogel; Naomi Kotkin and Caryl Levy, Uri's teachers from Gezah Daled at Beth El nursery school in New Rochelle; Beth El librarian Ruth Kaufmann; librarians Hazel Carp, Diane Braun, and Penny Eisenstein from Greenfield Hebrew Academy in Atlanta; our good friend, photographer Joel Silverman; Randee Friedman from Sounds Write Productions in San Diego; dance instructor Steven Weintraub in Atlanta; Janice Alper, Adelle Salmenson, and Rebecca Gordon from Jewish Educational Services in Atlanta; Dawne Bear at the Jewish Federation in San Francisco; Vicki Compter at UJA in New York; Rebecca Hoelting for her Atlanta contacts; Simon Amiel with Hillel in D.C.; Rachelle Bradt at the Yeshiva University Museum in New York; Israeli dance expert Judy Brown in Jerusalem; Rachel Glazer and Elaine Gitlin from Beth Tfiloh day school in Baltimore; Liz Wolf in Raleigh; Lauren Roman at craigNco in California; Harold Messinger in Austin; Ruth Goodman Burger from the Israeli Dance Institute in New York; Cantor Sharon Walloch in Baltimore; Vivian Ellison and Fran Cook from the Home Depot greenhouse in Atlanta; David Firooz from JewishStore.Com; Shlomo Lehavi at Hataklit in Los Angeles; The Judaica Corner in Atlanta; Westside Judaica in New York; Haim Scheininger at Sisu; Judye Groner and Madeline Wikler at Kar-Ben Copies; Susan Schwartz at Davka; Jeff Astor, Debbie, and Emanuel at T.E.S.; Joe Buchwald Gelles with JeMM; Debbie at Behrman House; Esther Netter and Sherri Kadovitz at the Zimmer Children's Museum in Los Angeles; Suzanne Hurwitz, Michelle Chepenik, Barbara Kreissman, Harry Stern, Kim Goodfriend, and Deborah Goldstein from the MJCC in Atlanta; Mark Greenberg at the Museum of the Southern Jewish Experience; Shari Rosenstein-Werb and Lynn Williams at the Holocaust Museum in D.C.; Cantor Tali Katz at the Jewish Museum of Maryland; Cantor Bob Fisher in Las Vegas; Lorin Sklamberg from Living Traditions; Shmuel Batzri from Dance Washington; Heather Johnson at the Jewish Museum San Francisco; Amy Berkowitz at Camp Tawonga; Ellen Barocas at NJY Camps; Ruth Shapira at Ramah in the Poconos; Laurie Kovens from the National Havurah Committee; Ellie Sandler at Spertus in Chicago; Aaron Katler with

Endangered Spirit; Irene Bennett with OSRUI; Miriam Rinn and Jason Black with the JCC Association of North America; Matt Schuman from Maccabi USA; Michelle Spivak with the Jewish War Veterans of USA; Bill Maurer from the Gomez Mill House.

Introduction

Teachers know well that a little fun can go a long way when it comes to kids and learning. The fact is, kids are learning all the time—everything they do is an experience that will play a part in shaping them as they grow. But the more an activity sparks children's imagination, the better the chance they will be fully engaged in it. And, by nature, if children are focused and enjoying themselves such that the experience is memorable, then the very best and truest form of learning has occurred.

Of course, *The Jewish Lights Book of Fun Classroom Activities* isn't designed to be a complete curriculum for teaching kids about Jewish life. The activities and materials described in here are just the icing on the cake of Jewish learning. They are no substitute for the teaching of basic and fundamental Jewish skills and concepts: Torah, Hebrew, holiday observances, values, and so on. But taken in conjunction with the fundamentals, this book can provide a welcome break from the more serious stuff, while reinforcing values and traditions already learned.

The Jewish Lights Book of Fun Classroom Activities hopes to impart the message that all activities—even everyday fun such as playing games, singing songs, or watering plants—can be Jewish activities if they're approached from a Jewish perspective. The goal of this book is to guide you toward a variety of terrific activities for kids and to inspire you to come up with your own Jewish fun ideas for your class.

As much as possible, we attempted to let the activities in this book speak for themselves; that is, we've provided a wide variety of accessible projects and materials with just enough background information to explain the relevance of each activity. In other words, less talk, more action. This way, classes are able to use these activities or adapt them any way they see fit. We've also included age ranges for each activity, but ultimately you are responsible for determining if an activity is appropriate for your students.

The book is divided into two sections:

- "Holiday Fun" includes crafts, recipes, activities, and unusual customs related to each holiday.

- "Classroom Fun for Anytime" has outdoor activities, games, and dances as well as ideas for "mitzvah" work and volunteerism; and extensive information on the best music, books, videos, computer software, and websites for Jewish classrooms.

You've read this far, so you're on the right track. But, as we said, this book is not just about *reading*—it's about *doing!* We hope you have as much fun using this book as we've had writing it.

Part I
Holiday Fun

1 Shabbat

While Shabbat is a day for Jewish kids to enjoy with their family, away from school, the classroom provides a great place to prepare for Shabbat—to impart the values and fun surrounding this weekly day of rest. Shabbat is a break from the chores and homework of the rest of the week, to rest and get rejuvenated so that we can be our best the other six days of the week. It's a time to do something special and enjoy quality time with loved ones.

Since Shabbat begins Friday evening and continues until Saturday evening, the school day on Friday is an ideal time to get kids into the Shabbat spirit. One great idea for Friday's Shabbat preparation is to go around the class and have everyone share something nice that happened to them that week or something nice they did for someone else. It's also a great time for special programs that involve singing (particularly Shabbat songs and prayers) and other fun activities. More than anything else, it's a great time to set the mood for Shabbat's most important activity: relaxing.

Hospitality: Mi Classroom es "Jew" Classroom

Hospitality is an old and important Jewish tradition. According to rabbinic teachings, it goes all the way back to Abraham and Sarah. He sat at the open flap of his tent waiting to welcome guests inside. She stood ready to fix a hot meal at a moment's notice. And neither of them would sit down to eat until they had tended to all of their guests.

This important Jewish principle applies all the time, not just on Shabbat and holidays. But since Shabbat comes every week and we're in less of a hurry, it gives us a regular opportunity to invite others over to visit. While we typically invite family and friends to our house, there's no reason we can't practice a little Shabbat hospitality in the classroom as well. Consider inviting guests—other classes, parents, or even members of the outside community—into your class for special Shabbat-oriented programs. And get the kids involved in determining whom to invite, what to serve (snacks or lunch), and what activities to do. They'll often come up with some great ideas.

By having guests, we share our traditions and open ourselves up to learn the customs of others. It makes Shabbat all the more special to have new faces, new voices, and new opinions involved. We benefit from it ourselves, and we're also bringing happiness to someone else. Everyone's a winner in the deal.

CAN-DO CANDLESTICKS
Ages 5–10

On Friday night, as Shabbat begins, traditionally a prayer is said as two candles are lit (see Appendix of Prayers, page 197). The idea is to have more light than usual—one flame for weeknights, two flames for Shabbat. However, some families light an extra candle for each child in the family. So it's always a great classroom activity to have the kids make extra candlesticks. Here's an easy way to make them out of clay.

WHAT YOU NEED:
Materials
- self-hardening clay
- Shabbat candle (for sizing)
- beads (optional)
- acrylic paint

Equipment
- forks (or other pointy utensils that aren't dangerous)
- paintbrushes (suitable for coating and for decorating)

HOW IT'S DONE:
1. Roll the clay into two balls the size of two small oranges—one for each candlestick.

2. Press each ball down into the newspaper to flatten the bottom while keeping the top part rounded.

3. Use your thumb to press a hole in the top center of each clay ball, about one inch deep. Put a Shabbat candle into the holes to make sure they are the right size. Remove candle before decorating.

4. Carve designs in the clay using the forks or other utensils. Write words like "Shabbat Shalom" in English or Hebrew (see Appendix of Stencils, page 208), or your family's names, or any type of designs you'd like.

5. If you choose to use beads, push them into the clay for extra decoration.

6. Allow the clay to harden overnight.

7. Paint the clay candlesticks. You may want to paint them one solid lighter color first, allow that to dry, then paint designs with darker colors on top of the first coat.

"KID-ISH" KIDDUSH CUP
Ages 4–9

It's nice for everyone at the Shabbat table (or pre-Shabbat classroom celebration on Friday) to have his or her own Kiddush cup for the traditional blessing over the wine or grape juice (see Appendix of Prayers, page 199). Kids can make these "stained glass" Kiddush cups all by themselves— either one for themselves, to use in class, or a bunch to bring home to their families.

WHAT YOU NEED:

Materials
- white glue
- water
- clear plastic cups (plastic goblets are best)
- colored tissue paper, cut in different small shapes
- shellac

Equipment
- old or disposable bowl
- paintbrushes (for spreading glue and for shellac)

HOW IT'S DONE:

1. Using a paintbrush, mix together equal parts glue and water in the bowl.

2. Paint the glue/water mixture on the entire outside of the cup.

3. With your fingers, stick the pieces of tissue paper onto the cup, overlapping them and smoothing them down until you cover the entire cup. (The glue will soften the tissue paper.)

4. Brush the glue onto the entire cup again, over the layer of tissue paper.

5. Allow the cup to dry overnight. It will dry clear, and the tissue paper will let the light shine through the cup like stained glass.

6. Put a coat of shellac over the whole cup to seal your creation. (This should be done by an adult.)

7. After it dries, you can drink wine or grape juice out of it. Then rinse it out by hand; don't put it in a dishwasher.

DANIELLE'S DOUGH-LICIOUS SHABBAT MINI-CHALLAH
Ages 3 and up

The braided egg bread known as challah is something special. Yes, you can eat challah anytime, and you can eat any kind of bread on Shabbat. But come on, what would Shabbat be without challah? And if it's homemade—or even classroom-made—even better!

Baking in class, of course, presents certain logistical challenges, and there are safety considerations as well. While most classrooms will not have an oven for baking, schools will usually allow teachers (though not children) access to the kitchen. This simply means students can be involved in the preparation of the recipe but may not be able to experience the actual baking.

Once you have your *challot* (the plural of challah) ready to eat, don't forget to cover them when they're on the dinner table. It's as if we are protecting the challah's feelings, since the blessing over the bread comes last, after the prayers for the candles, wine, and washing of the hands (see Appendix of Prayers, pages 197, 199).

Note: This recipe makes enough dough for about four kid-sized mini-*challot;* multiply all ingredients according to the number of students. Rather than having each child mix his or her own dough, we recommend that four to eight students help in mixing a (single or double) batch, then break the dough into fist-sized portions for braiding by each child.

WHAT YOU NEED:

Materials

- 1 egg at room temperature
- ¾ cup warm water
- 2 tbsp oil
- 1 tsp lemon juice
- 2 cups bread flour
- 1 tsp salt
- 2½ tbsp sugar
- 1 tbsp gluten (found in most health food stores)
- 1 tsp active dry yeast
- ¼ cup raisins (optional)
- wash: 1 egg yolk, beaten, and 1 tbsp water
- topping: sesame or poppy seeds (optional)

Utensils

- bread machine or large bowl
- measuring cup
- measuring spoons
- bread board or smooth surface

HOW IT'S DONE:

1. Mix all the ingredients in a large bowl (except for toppings and "wash" ingredients). With lightly floured hands, kids can take turns kneading the dough until it is completely blended.

2. Cover the bowl with a towel and set in a warm place for one hour to allow the dough to rise.

3. Knead a little bit more, and then distribute portions to each student.

4. Each student should divide his or her dough into three equal parts for braiding.

5. Roll the three parts into ropes of equal length, and lay them parallel to each other.

6. Pinch the top ends together to join them. Braid the ropes. Then pinch the bottom ends together.

7. Place the pieces of braided dough on a shallow baking pan (allow enough space between each for expansion while baking), cover the dough with damp paper towels, and let the dough rise.

8. After the dough has risen for a half hour, preheat oven to 375°F.

9. About 15 minutes later, when the dough has doubled in size, students can combine the "wash" ingredients and brush it onto their braids. They can also sprinkle their braids with poppy or sesame seeds.

10. Place mini-*challot* in oven and bake for 20–25 minutes or until golden brown.

THE "SUPER-APPEALING, SPILL-CONCEALING" TABLECLOTH
Ages 3–9

Creating a tablecloth is not only a fun craft for kids, but their families can use the creation for years to come. If you use fabric paint or permanent markers on the cloth, the tablecloth will be safe to throw into a washing machine.

(A smaller version of this project makes a great challah cover. Since they don't have to be washed as often, feel free to get fancy and sew on all sorts of beads and gold trim. *Special tip:* Colorful tablecloths and challah covers are good for hiding wine and grape juice spills.)

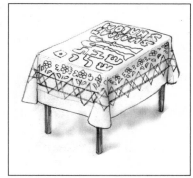

WHAT YOU NEED:
- white sheet (or handkerchief for a challah cover)
- fabric markers or fabric paint

HOW IT'S DONE:

1. With the fabric paint or markers, draw a simple design around the borders of the cloth. It can be Jewish stars, flowers, or anything the kids would like to draw.

2. In the middle of the cloth, write "Shabbat Shalom" in English or Hebrew (see Appendix of Stencils, page 208), and draw Shabbat-related symbols: candles, a Kiddush cup, challah, and Jewish stars. Children can also use stencils to get the designs just right.

3. Allow the paint or ink from the markers to completely dry before using.

Out with a Bang! Havdalah Fun

On Saturday evenings, the Havdalah ceremony (which can be conducted at home or in synagogue) marks the end of Shabbat and the beginning of the regular week. We wish one another a good week ahead and reflect on the one gone by. During this beautiful ceremony, we use a braided candle, wine, and great-smelling spices (called *besamim* in Hebrew). A wonderful way to prepare for this service during the week is to create *besamim* spices and a container to hold them.

MAKING YOUR OWN *BESAMIM* BOX

Ages 4–10

The spice box, or *besamim* box, can be made out of any kind of fairly airtight container. The lid should lift or open to allow everyone to smell what's inside.

A fun and simple way to make a *besamim* box is to use a large sliding matchbox (or kids can use a small matchbox for a tiny *besamim* holder). Once you've found the perfect boxes, students need only decorate them.

One idea for decorating the *besamim* box is to paste on bits of colored construction paper and then cover it with clear contact paper (or just clear tape) to laminate it. Or kids can paint their boxes, or cover them with cloth or just about any other material. If using matchboxes, be sure to cover up the striker part of the boxes so they don't pose a threat.

When students are done decorating, one final piece will make it a little easier to slide their boxes open and closed: have them glue a bead onto the end of the inner, sliding box to create a knob on the little drawer. Then they can put their spices inside and slide out the drawer for Havdalah—or whenever they want—to take a whiff.

SOME EASY-TO-GROW HERBS FOR YOUR *BESAMIM* BOX

All ages

Both mint and rosemary have a fragrant, strong smell. English lavender also smells great, and it has pretty little purple flowers. All are easy to grow, either inside, by the classroom window, or outside, if your school has a garden area. (But be sure to plant *English* lavender. Other kinds are more fussy.)

The great thing about all three plants is that once they have been planted, they'll stay around a while. Depending upon your local climate, you may not see them during the winter if you plant them outside. Yet rest assured they're still there. Because they're perennials they will come back once the weather warms up.

You can get the plants inexpensively at a garden center and plant them either in the garden or in pots. Make sure the plants get plenty of light and stay moist, and they will soon take root and flourish.

2 Rosh Hashanah & Yom Kippur

Happy New Year! Rosh Hashanah, which usually falls in September, marks the beginning of the Jewish year. It's a time of joy and celebration—of blowing the shofar to alert everyone to this important holiday—and of eating sweets like apples and honey in hopes of a sweet year.

The ten-day period between Rosh Hashanah and Yom Kippur (the Day of Atonement) is the climax of a month-long introspective period, when we think about changes we'd like to make for the year to come. The idea is that by the end of Yom Kippur, we should feel completely rejuvenated and ready to embrace the possibilities of a new year. That takes some work, though: we must apologize to those we've wronged, admit to ourselves the mistakes we've made, and decide to make some necessary changes—effective immediately. Unlike the secular new year—when the tradition is to party hard and worry about new year's resolutions the next day—Jewish tradition recognizes that change doesn't come so easily and therefore needs to be the focal point of the celebration.

Rosh Hashanah is a great time for students to reflect together and make new year's resolutions. Encourage kids to think about things they might have done wrong and to whom they may owe apologies. By Yom Kippur, they should have devised a plan to avoid making the same mistakes in the new year. As the holiday liturgy puts it: "On Rosh Hashanah it is written, and on Yom Kippur it is sealed...."

While Rosh Hashanah and Yom Kippur observance is clearly a time for reflection and discussion, let's not become so obsessed with the importance of the holidays that we lose sight of the joy involved

in welcoming the new year. If we do, we miss the point entirely—
to brighten our own lives and the lives of the people around us.

TOOTING YOUR OWN SHOFAR
Ages 5–9

The shofar is blown at synagogue each
morning for the entire month before
Rosh Hashanah. Kids absolutely love
to hear the sound of the shofar, so it's
nice to also have one in the classroom
as well. Even more than hearing it,
kids are thrilled to get the chance to
blow it themselves.

Unless you know how to play the trumpet, getting a shofar to
make noise is not so easy to do. So students and teachers alike
tend to be delightfully surprised when they actually hear a sound
come out. It's then that the shofar best fulfills its role as a "Jewish
alarm clock": jolting us, waking us up, and reminding us to think
about the past year and how we can make the next one better for
everyone.

In biblical times, the shofar—made then, as now, from a ram's
horn—was used to announce important arrivals or warn of enemies approaching. At over four thousand years old and counting,
it's one of the oldest and most enduring musical instruments.

In case your class can't get a real shofar—or it's too difficult for
the kids to blow—here's a great toy substitute you can make that'll
get everyone in the class to "wake up and smell the new year!"

WHAT YOU NEED:

Materials
- plastic party horn (mouthpiece only)
- paper plate
- crayons or markers
- glitter glue (optional)

Equipment
- scissors
- clear plastic tape

HOW IT'S DONE:

1. Fold a paper plate in half.

2. Cut out the shape of a shofar. (You'll have two shofar-shaped pieces.)

3. Color and decorate the two shofar pieces with crayons and markers. You can write *"Shanah Tovah"* (good year) in English or Hebrew with crayons, markers, or glitter glue (see Appendix of Stencils, page 209). Allow the shofar pieces to dry if necessary.

4. Tape the top and bottom edges of the two pieces together to create a horn-shaped paper shofar.

5. Insert the plastic party horn into the small opening of the shofar, so that the mouthpiece is sticking out slightly, and tape it in place.

6. Toot your horn!

Have someone call out the name of the four different sounds made with the shofar before you make that sound:

- *Tekiah*—one long blast

- *Teruah*—three medium blasts

- *Shevarim*—nine short (staccato) blasts

- *Tekiah Gedolah*—a final very long blast (as long as you can hold your breath!)

TASHLICH: TOSSING YOUR COOKIES FOR THE NEW YEAR
All ages

Tashlich (which means "you shall cast [away]" in Hebrew) is a brief ceremony, usually done on the afternoon of the first day of Rosh Hashanah, that involves standing beside a body of water (for example, the local lake or stream) and throwing whatever bread crumbs we have in our pockets into the water. (Given that most of us don't already have pockets filled with bread crumbs, we bring bread or cookie crumbs with us.) The idea is symbolic: to purge ourselves of our sins, clean ourselves out, and make a fresh start. *Tashlich* is a physical way for us all to convey what we're trying to accomplish spiritually at this time of year. It's meaningful not only for adults but also for kids (especially if they can use their "sins" to feed the ducks).

Synagogues will sometimes plan a group trip to a nearby body of water to do *Tashlich*, which includes a few Bible quotations, readings, and songs. However, the custom can also be a fun class excursion for one of the days leading up to Rosh Hashanah. And if your school isn't located near a body of water, you can simply have your students stand beside a classroom sink. Before they throw their crumbs into the water, have students visualize which specific acts the crumbs represent. Encourage kids to picture themselves throwing those acts into the water so they won't do them again.

INSIDE-OUT CANDIED APPLE

Ages 7 and up

A very common Rosh Hashanah tradition is to eat apples dipped in honey to get a sweet start to the new year. (For a new year's blessing, see Appendix of Prayers, page 203). For a fun in-class treat, here's a way to use the apple as a dipping bowl for the honey:

WHAT YOU NEED:

Ingredients
- apples
- lemon juice
- honey (or caramel)

Utensils
- paring knife (for use by grown-ups only)
- pretty plate

HOW IT'S DONE:

1. After washing an apple, core it like a Halloween pumpkin by cutting from the top and hollowing out the insides. (An adult

should do this.) Do not cut or pierce the sides or bottom of the apple. (You're turning it into a cup to hold the honey.)

2. Rinse the inside of the apple with lemon juice to help prevent it from turning brown.

3. Fill the center of the apple with honey.

4. Place the apple cup in the center of the plate. Slice up another apple or two, and lay the pieces around the apple cup on the plate.

5. Pass the plate around and enjoy.

OLD COUNTRY NUT 'N' HONEY TREATS
Ages 7 and up

Another traditional honey-related Rosh Hashanah treat is *taiglach*, honey candies that originated in Eastern Europe. The name is Yiddish for "many pieces of dough." Here's a recipe for *taiglach* that makes about 40 pieces of candy (adjust quantities as needed). Kids can help in mixing the ingredients and rolling the "rope" before baking, and then in wrapping the candy after it has cooled.

WHAT YOU NEED:

Ingredients
- 2 eggs (lightly beaten)
- 2 tbsp vegetable oil, plus enough to grease the pan
- 1½ cups flour
- ½ tsp salt
- ¾ tsp baking powder
- 1 cup honey
- ½ cup sugar
- ½ tsp ground ginger
- 1 cup nuts (coarsely chopped)

Utensils
- shallow baking pan
- mixing bowls
- whisk or fork
- stirring spoons
- board (or other smooth surface for rolling dough)
- saucepan
- large platter
- waxed paper
- measuring cups

HOW IT'S DONE:

1. Preheat oven to 375°F. Grease the pan well and set it aside.

2. Mix the eggs and oil in a bowl. In a separate bowl, sift together the flour, salt, and baking powder. Combine the two mixtures, and stir to make dough that is soft but not sticky. Add more flour if necessary.

3. Lightly sprinkle a board with flour. Place the dough on it. With lightly floured hands, twist the dough into a rope about ½ inch thick. Dip a knife in flour, and cut the rope of dough into small pieces about ½ inch long.

4. Place the pieces into the baking pan, and bake for about 10 minutes or until slightly browned. Shake the pan a few times to keep the pieces separated and evenly browned.

5. To prepare the honey syrup, put the honey, sugar, and ginger in a saucepan. Stir until the sugar is completely melted. Cook it over a low flame for 5 minutes, stirring constantly so the honey doesn't burn.

6. Add the baked pieces of dough and the nuts into the pan. Stir gently over a low heat until the mixture is a deep golden brown.

7. Using cold water, wet a large platter or board. Pour the coated pieces onto it. When the candy is cool, wrap the pieces individually in waxed paper.

A ROSH HASHANAH SEDER
Ages 6 and up

Sephardic and Persian Hors D'Oeuvres

Sephardic and Persian Jews have a great Rosh Hashanah tradition involving a bunch of different foods, each symbolizing a certain good omen for the new year. This Rosh Hashanah seder is a terrific classroom activity for the days leading up to the holiday, or the days between Rosh Hashanah and Yom Kippur. A special Hebrew prayer goes along with each item. Unlike other prayers for food, during this seder we're not thanking God for the food specifically; we're using these symbolic foods to ask God for a good year ahead.

Below we've included passages from the prayers that explain the connections made. (For a complete list of these prayers, see pages 203–207). Say the prayer for each item, or simply discuss the item's significance. Then pass around the foods, and enjoy.

1. Apples dipped in honey: "May it be a sweet year."

2. Steamed leeks: "May all evil in the world be cut off." (Leeks grow like grass, and they're cut when harvested.)

3. Steamed or boiled beets: "May all evil in the world be wiped out." (The beet, which grows in the ground, is uprooted and must be cleaned off before we eat it.)

4. Dates: "I am God's servant." (Dates are among the biblical fruits from the Land of Israel; they represent the sweetness of the relationship between God and the Jewish people.)

5. Zucchini or squash: "Tear up the evil decree against us." (This prayer talks about starting over and planting the seeds of goodness for a new year. Zucchini and squash, which are full of seeds, must be replanted every year.)

6. Beans: "May our merits and our inspirations multiply" (like the number of beans produced from just one plant).

7. Pomegranate: "May we be as full of *mitzvot* (good deeds) as the pomegranate is full of seeds."

8. Fish: "May our merits multiply like fish in the sea."

9. Something from the head of an animal: "May we be in the forefront like the head and not in the background like the tail." (This prayer is reminding us that we should be leaders and not followers.) Sephardim have used a fish head, perhaps because they lived near the water. But the prayer really calls for something from a ram's head "in remembrance of the ram that replaced Isaac."

A Persian twist: Iranian Jews do this same ceremony with slight modifications:

2. The leeks are eaten raw for this ceremony. Persians hold a bunch of grass-like leek strands with both hands (one hand at each end) and say the prayer. Then they take a bite out of the middle and throw the remaining ends over their shoulders; what's in the left hand goes over the right shoulder, and what's in the right hand goes over the left shoulder. This furthers the theme of "May all evil in the world be cut off" with a symbolic gesture of "divide and conquer."

8. The Persians substitute lung for the fish. The prayer says, "May our sins be light like the lung." (The meat from lung is very light meat.) You can special order it from some kosher butchers.

9. While the Sephardim have used a fish head, Persians usually use the tongue of a lamb or cow. (Fish wasn't as readily available in Persia as it was in Spain. This might be the reason for both these changes in steps 8 and 9.)

SENDING THE VERY BEST NEW YEAR'S CARDS
Ages 4–11

Everyone loves getting cards for Rosh Hashanah, and personally made cards are the best kind. Students can wish a good new year (*Shanah Tovah*, in Hebrew) to parents, grandparents, aunts and uncles, cousins, friends, even teachers. (To go along with these cards, make your own envelopes, too. See the instructions in the section on Arts & Crafts, pages 121–122).

WHAT YOU NEED:
Materials

- colored construction paper
- white paper
- glue
- sponges or potatoes (for paint stamps)
- paper towels, stamp pad, ink, or tempera paint (for stamps)
- reprints of a nice family photo
- collage items: pictures from other cards or magazines

Equipment
- markers and crayons
- scissors and/or knife (for teacher's use only)

HOW IT'S DONE:

1. Fold a piece of colored construction paper in half.

2. Your piece of white paper should be slightly smaller than your construction paper. Fold it in half as well. (It will eventually be glued to the inside of the folded construction paper.)

3. Write a message on the white paper. Include a *Shanah Tovah* wish in either English or Hebrew (see Appendix of Stencils, page 209) and some decorations, along with whatever message the student would like to include.

4. Decorate the paper with drawings, using markers or crayons. In addition to (or instead of) drawings, you can also make a paint-stamp to use for decoration: Teachers can either cut shapes (such as a Jewish star) out of a sponge or carve shapes from one end of a halved potato—using the rest of the potato as a handle. If you don't have an ink pad, then make your own by soaking some paper towels in paint. Press the stamp onto the pad and then onto the white paper.

5. After the decorations dry, glue the white paper with the new year's message onto the inside of the card.

6. On the outside of the card, have students make a collage using pieces of other *Shanah Tovah* cards or pictures from magazines.

HISTORY IN THE MAKING: DESIGNING YOUR OWN JEWISH CALENDAR
Ages 9 and up

Since Rosh Hashanah is the start of the new year, it's also the time to start a new calendar. These do-it-yourself calendars are great school projects and also make for great gifts.

WHAT YOU NEED:

Materials
- white paper (which you'll photocopy at least 12 times)
- colored construction paper (at least 12 sheets)
- glue
- yarn

Equipment
- ruler
- pencil
- hole puncher
- markers or paint
- calendar that includes Jewish holidays to use as a model

HOW IT'S DONE:

1. Make a grid for the calendar pages. To do this, take a blank piece of paper and, with a pencil, draw six equally spaced vertical lines down the page and four equally spaced horizontal lines across the page. You'll end up with a grid of 7 boxes across and 5 down, for a total of 35 boxes on the page.

2. Photocopy this sheet 12 times for each student (plus a few extra in case you make mistakes while filling them in). Teachers may want to do these first two steps before class and have the pages ready to go.

3. Glue each grid onto a larger sheet of colored construction paper, leaving enough room at the top for you to write the days of the week—above that, the name of the month—in both English and Hebrew. (Remember that Jewish months do not begin and end on the same days as secular months, so it's likely that parts of two Hebrew months will appear within one secular month.)

4. Write the names of the days at the top of each of the seven columns, from Sunday *(Yom Rishon)* to Saturday (Shabbat).

5. Refer to a store-bought calendar for the same year to see on which day the secular and Jewish months begin, how many days are in each month, and on which days Jewish and secular holidays fall. (Start the calendar with whichever secular month

Rosh Hashanah falls in this year—usually September.) Fill out the grid by writing the date in each box where a date should go. (Remember that each month probably starts on a different day of the week than the month before it.) Wherever a holiday occurs, draw a picture that corresponds to that holiday. Also mark any birthdays and anniversaries of family members and close friends that occur in that month.

6. Repeat the process in steps four and five with each of the remaining months.

7. Punch 5 holes along the top of the 12 sheets of paper, making sure the holes line up when the pages are stacked. Thread yarn through the holes to fasten the sheets together. Also, punch a hole at the bottom of the calendar (lining up on every page) so that you can hang the calendar open on the wall.

8. When the fastened calendar lies open to a particular month, the bottom page will contain the calendar while the top will be blank (it's the back of the previous month). To further decorate your calendar, you can draw pictures or paste photos on this page.

3 Sukkot

Sukkot, which begins four days after Yom Kippur, is one of the best holidays for active classroom participation. Because the festival lasts a full eight days and not all the days are *khagim* (major holidays, where Jews would not typically go to school), there's a good chance you'd be able to have a Sukkot activity in class on one of the actual days of the holiday. The most primary Sukkot activity is building a *sukkah*, a hut where Jews eat during the seven days of this holiday.

The festival of Sukkot has two origins. Historically, it commemorates the Israelites' forty years of wandering in the wilderness, when they built temporary shelters to live in. Agriculturally, Sukkot celebrates the end of the harvest season and recalls the type of temporary dwellings our ancestors built out in the fields, where they'd stay while harvesting.

If possible, have your class participate in the building and/or decorating of a *sukkah*. And once it has been erected, try to spend time in the *sukkah*—for meals or special holiday-related activities. We can take this hut and turn it into a magical place. For a week, the *sukkah* becomes a special area for family, friends, and classmates to spend valuable time together.

The *sukkah* also represents the unpredictability of life. It can be blown away in an instant if a big, unexpected wind comes along. With that in mind, this is a perfect time to discuss the issue of homelessness with your class: what it would be like to live all year around with so little shelter (or none at all).

SUKKAH-BUILDING BASICS
All ages

Sukkahs come in all shapes and sizes, but there are a few rules about how to construct them. The two main rules are these:

1. A *sukkah* has to have at least three walls (one of which can be an existing wall, like the side of the house).

2. The roof needs to provide mostly shade yet leave enough openings so you can see stars through it at night. Most commonly the roof is made out of *skhach,* tree branches or twigs, which suits both needs perfectly. However, it can be made out of any organic material as long as it's not something permanent, such as bricks or wood boards.

For an even simpler solution, many synagogues and Jewish gift shops sell *sukkah*-making kits with all the necessary materials (except tools) and directions for building the frame. They're usually pretty easy to put together.

TIPS FOR THE *SUKKAH* "INTERIOR DECORATOR"
All ages

Unlike the guidelines for constructing the *sukkah,* there aren't any rules for decorating inside; it's pretty much anything goes! But because the *sukkah* is exposed to the elements, fragile decorations won't keep well—particularly those that fall apart or run when they get wet. Here are a few *sukkah* decoration tips:

Sturdy vegetables and fruit Dried gourds, Indian corn, and pumpkins are available at this time of year and make great *sukkah* decorations. You can hang small ones from the roof with string and lay bigger ones in the corner. (You can also use artificial fruit. Fresh fruit isn't the greatest, since it can rot and attract bugs.)

Paper chains Take strips of construction paper and glue them into loops that are linked together to make paper chains. Similarly, you can make decorative chains by stringing together old plastic foam packing pieces (peanuts). For a fancier touch, pretreat the pieces with gold and silver paint. You can also hang colorful strands of beads, like old necklaces (or Mardi Gras beads).

Artwork All kinds of paintings or drawings make nice *sukkah* decorations. You can hang special *sukkah* artwork that the kids make in class. Paintings of different types of fruit are especially good. Protect them from getting wet with plastic wrap or clear contact paper.

Ushpizin This term, which means "visitors," refers to the mystical custom of inviting a different aspect of God into the *sukkah* each day. Some contemporary Jews have extended this practice to include inviting people important to us who are no longer living yet are with us in spirit. We decorate the *sukkah* with pictures of our loved ones, role models, and heroes—anyone from biblical patriarchs and matriarchs, to family members who have passed away, to those people we admire like Martin Luther King, Jr. or Anne Frank. With these photos or drawings hanging in our *sukkah,* we invite them all to be with us as we celebrate. Ask for your students' participation in picking *ushpizin,* or have them bring in pictures (copies, preferably, in case they get lost or damaged) of their ancestors or heroes.

Table decorations Every *sukkah* should have a table and chairs so that meals can be eaten inside. Specially decorated tablecloths, challah covers, and Kiddush cups add a warm and special feel to the *sukkah* (see the "Shabbat" section, pages 3–11).

SUKKAH-IN-A-*SUKKAH* CENTERPIECE
Ages 4–8

Since eating meals is an important *sukkah* activity, table centerpieces offer another opportunity for decoration. (Or, if you aren't able to build a *sukkah* at school, this can be a symbolic way of "building" a *sukkah* for kids to take home with them.)

WHAT YOU NEED:

Materials
- shoebox (without lid)
- twigs with leaves (preferably evergreen)
- old magazines with pictures of fruit

Equipment
- tempera paints
- scissors (for teacher's use only in younger classes)
- paintbrushes
- glue

HOW IT'S DONE:

1. Draw a door on one side of the box, and cut it out. Or you can completely cut off one side of the box, because a *sukkah* only has to have three walls.

2. Paint the sides of the box with pictures of fruit, or glue on pictures of fruit that you cut out of magazines.

3. Place twigs with leaves across the open top of the box to complete the mini-*sukkah* centerpiece.

4. If you want to get really creative, make a mini-table to put inside your mini-*sukkah* (and put a mini-mini-*sukkah* table centerpiece on it).

All Shook Up! The *Lulav* and *Etrog*

In addition to the *sukkah,* another fun Sukkot custom is the shaking of the *lulav* and *etrog. Lulav* means "palm branch," but the *lulav* we traditionally use is actually made up of two smaller willow branches plus three small myrtle branches, all bound together. The *etrog* is a citron fruit; it has a great smell and looks like a big bumpy lemon. We hold these together and shake them firmly in a set pattern as a way of commemorating the holiday.

The *lulav* and *etrog* have symbolic significance relating to parts of the human body: the *etrog* represents the heart (being true); the *lulav* represents the spine (being straight with ourselves and others); the willow represents the lips (being careful what we say); and the myrtle represents the eyes (noticing what's important). Most synagogues have one or more *lulav* and *etrog* sets at this time of year that you can use in their communal *sukkah*. Or you can buy your own *lulav* and *etrog* (ask your synagogue or nearby Judaica shop at least a week before Sukkot begins).

THE REAL-DEAL *LULAV* SHAKE

All ages

By shaking the *lulav* and *etrog* around us, we symbolically surround ourselves with Sukkot on all sides and bring it toward us. Hold the *lulav* in your right hand and the *etrog* in your left, with both hands touching each other. Stand facing the east as you say the special prayer (see Appendix of Prayers, page 201), and then follow these steps:

1. Hold the assembled *lulav*-and-*etrog* directly out in front of you, then shake it (deliberately, so that it rattles) toward your body three times.

2. Hold the *lulav*-and-*etrog* to your right, and shake it toward your body three times.

3. Hold the *lulav*-and-*etrog* over your shoulder so it is behind you, and shake it back toward you three times.

4. Hold the *lulav*-and-*etrog* to your left, and shake it toward your body three times.

THE WACKY 'N' TASTY *LULAV* "SHAKE"
All ages

After your students take turns shaking the assembled *lulav*-and-*etrog*, a fun nontraditional Sukkot treat is to create a different, delicious kind of shake: an ice-cream shake. Just mix a favorite kind of ice cream with some milk in a blender (the kids can help with the mixing, but the teacher should be the only one to operate the blender). To symbolize the *lulav* and *etrog* (since we wouldn't actually want to eat these things!), green and/or yellow flavors of ice cream are best (lime, lemon, or mint flavors), or you can add food coloring to a vanilla shake. After you pour the shake into cups, students can decorate them with a few small branches that have been washed clean (to represent the *lulav*) and some yellow candy-coated chocolates or lemon drops sprinkled on top (to represent the *etrog*). Add a straw and spoon, then start slurping!

4 Simchat Torah

Right after Sukkot is the holiday of Simchat Torah. After a whole year of reading a section of the Torah each week in synagogue, on Simchat Torah we celebrate because the cycle is finished. And now that it's done, what's next? Naturally, we start again! But not before we have a little fun first.

While the adults are the ones who read from the Torah, Simchat Torah is also a children's holiday. At synagogue, there's singing and dancing for all ages, and candy is given out. Plus, this is the only holiday when kids come up to the Torah to make a blessing (an *aliyah*), an honor usually reserved for people older than bar and bat mitzvah age.

During services for Simchat Torah, everyone parades around the synagogue and even out into the street. Adults carry Torah scrolls while kids carry mini-Torah replicas or wave flags. Second only to Purim in its wild celebrating, Simchat Torah is a rare opportunity when having a party during services is not only acceptable, it's entirely appropriate.

While the nature of Simchat Torah's revelry requires that it take place during synagogue services rather than in the classroom, there are some preparations that can be done in class. Here are some ideas:

TINY TOTIN' TORAH SCROLLS

Ages 5–9

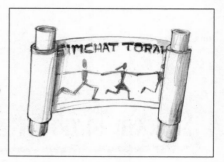

Here's a way for students to make their very own mini-Torah to carry when parading and dancing on Simchat Torah.

WHAT YOU NEED:

Materials
- 2 empty paper towel rolls
- 2 or 3 sheets of white paper
- 1 strip of cloth (about the length of a shoelace)

Equipment
- paint (including gold or silver)
- clear tape, glue, or a stapler
- markers
- paintbrushes

HOW IT'S DONE:

1. Paint the paper towel rolls, using at least a touch of gold or silver paint on the ends.

2. Using clear tape at the bottom and top of each piece of paper, attach two or three pieces of white paper together, end to end, to make one long sheet.

3. Glue or tape one end of the long paper sheet to each of the paper towel rolls. (If it doesn't hold well enough, you can staple it by sliding the stapler's bottom piece into the tube.)

4. Decorate the paper with words, stories, or pictures related to Simchat Torah or about being Jewish.

5. When the decorations are finished, roll up the scroll.

6. Tie the strip of cloth around the scroll to hold the paper towel rolls together.

FUN FLAGS FOR THE SIMCHAH STRUT
Ages 4–7

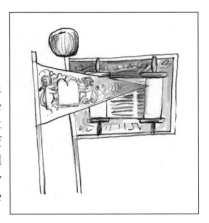

Besides mini-Torah scrolls, kids often wave flags as they dance and parade around the synagogue on Simchat Torah. There's even a tradition of sticking an apple (or a candied apple) on the top of a (relatively thick) flagstick. Here's how to make a flag.

WHAT YOU NEED:

Materials
- poster board
- wooden dowel rod or stick

Equipment
- glue
- decorations: glitter, markers, tempera or poster paint

HOW IT'S DONE:

1. Make your flag in the shape of a rectangle or a triangle. Cut whichever shape you choose out of the poster board.

2. Decorate the shape by drawing and coloring designs such as Torah scrolls and Jewish stars. Leave an inch or two of one side undecorated—this is where you'll glue the poster board to the stick.

3. Once the decorations dry, run a line of glue down the side of the flag. Lay the dowel flat on the glue, and leave it until it dries.

4. Start waving!

5 Hanukkah

anukkah is not a major festival in the Jewish religious calendar, but it's well known as a holiday that's a lot of fun. Plus,
there are important messages to be learned in the Hanukkah
story.

This eight-day holiday celebrates the miracles in the story of the
military victory of the Hasmonean Jews, led by Judah Maccabee,
over Syrian government forces in 164 B.C.E. It's the perfect winter
holiday—a festival of light at the darkest time of year.

Because Hanukkah falls close to Christmas, during the past century the holiday has become largely associated with gift-giving in
countries where most people are Christian. Gift-giving, however,
isn't what this holiday is traditionally about. Since a big part of
being Jewish is understanding how we are different, Hanukkah
actually provides a great chance to talk with your class about that
aspect of Judaism. It's important to recognize that being different
is not a bad thing if we understand, enjoy, and take pride in our
own holidays and customs—and respect the traditions of others as
well.

Consider having a fun activity planned for each school day
during Hanukkah: Read Hanukkah-related books such as the story
of the Maccabees; spend time creating gifts for the kids' friends,
family, or fellow students (a poem, song, or craft); play the dreidel game; design a menorah; cook up some latkes (potato pancakes) or *soofganiyot* (jelly donuts). Or have a Hanukkah party and
do them all!

MIRACULOUS MENORAH MAKING

Ages 4–12

The menorah (or *hanukiyah,* in modern Hebrew) is the eight-cupped oil lamp or eight-branch candelabra that we light each night of Hanukkah. It actually has nine candles if you count the *shamash,* the helper candle usually set apart from the rest of the menorah and used to light all the other candles.

The story goes that after the Maccabees' victory, the Temple needed to be rededicated because it had been wrecked by the Greeks. There was only enough ritually pure olive oil left in the Temple's menorah to burn for one day, but the priest went ahead and lit its lamps anyway. The lamps miraculously burned for eight days, during which time they were able to purify more oil.

The Hanukkah menorah remembers this miracle. We light one candle the first night of Hanukkah, two the next night, and so on. Families can light as many menorahs as they'd like, so kids will enjoy making their own in class to use during their family candlelighting. Here's an idea of how to create a variety of different menorahs.

WHAT YOU NEED:

Materials
- ceramic tile, wood, or metal (for the base)
- 10 metal lug nuts; or 10 sea shells (all similarly saucer-shaped); or 10 walnut shell halves (carefully broken); or 10 bottle caps

Equipment
- glue
- nonflammable decorations: paint, permanent markers, glitter glue, beads, small dreidels

HOW IT'S DONE:

1. Find something solid for the base of your menorah. This can be anything from ceramic tile to a nice piece of wood or a

piece of metal, as long as it's big enough to fit all your candleholders on it. (They should be spaced far enough apart that the flames appear distinct when viewed from outside your window.)

2. Decide what you are going to use to hold each of the candles on the menorah: lug nuts, shells, bottle caps, or any other idea you come up with. You'll need 10 of whatever you choose: 1 for each of the 8 candles, plus the *shamash* needs 2 stacked on top of each other (to make it taller than the rest so that it stands out).

3. Glue the candleholders to the base in whatever pattern you choose. Traditionally, all the candles are in a straight line—it's easier to light the menorah that way—but it can also look interesting to use a squiggly or circular pattern. Usually the *shamash* is placed in the middle or at one end.

4. Decorate the menorah any way that you want: with paints, markers, glitter glue, beads, or all of the above. You can paint your name on it, glue dreidels to it, or make pictures of just about anything you'd like.

Spinning and Winning: Dreidels and Gelt

Legend has it that at one point when the Syrian king Antiochus had control of the Land of Israel, he forbade prayer and the study of Torah. Some Jews responded by sneaking out to remote caves to study and pray, and whenever they saw soldiers coming they would quickly put away their books, pull out spinning tops, and pretend they were gambling. This way, the soldiers would think the Jews had simply sneaked away to gamble, which was not a serious crime like praying.

Today, we continue to play with those spinning tops—*dreidel* in English (from the Yiddish word for "turn"), *s'vivon* in Hebrew—to remember what our ancestors had to go through to practice their religion. Plus, we play because it's fun!

DREIDEL-PLAYING BASICS: HOW TO BE A GELT-SHARK

Ages 4 and up

Dreidel is best when it's played for "high stakes"; that is, for pieces of chocolate Hanukkah gelt. Let's explain:

Gelt is the Yiddish word for money. But when people talk about Hanukkah gelt these days, often they're referring to pieces of chocolate that are wrapped in gold foil, made to look like ancient coins. The tradition of Hanukkah gelt is said to go back to the Maccabees. After they defeated the enemy and became the rulers of Israel, they minted coins so the Jews could have their own currency. Perhaps that's why in later centuries, before gift-giving was customary, kids would sometimes get real coins as part of the Hanukkah celebration.

To play dreidel, you must pay attention to the letter written on each of its four sides. The letters on the dreidel refer to the miracle of Hanukkah: The letter *nun* stands for *nes* (miracle), the letter *gimmel* stands for *gadol* (big), the letter *hay* stands for *hayah* (happened), and the letter *shin* stands for *sham* (there, meaning in the Land of Israel). (And in Israel, the fourth letter on the dreidel is the letter *pay*, which stands for *po*, meaning "here"—"A great miracle happened *here*.")

However, when it comes to the dreidel game, the letters mean something else entirely. Players sit in a circle. Each person puts one or two pieces of Hanukkah gelt into the center. Then the dreidel is passed around the circle, and each player takes a turn spinning it. When the dreidel stops spinning, whichever letter is facing up determines what the player who spun it should do:

- If it stops on *nun*, then "nothing" happens; the next player goes.

- If it stops on *gimmel*, the player who spun "gets everything" in the center. Then everyone has to put in their entry amount again to continue.

- If it stops on *hay,* the player who spun takes "half" of what's in the center.

- If it stops on *shin,* the player who spun has to "shell out" one piece of gelt to the center.

Hanukkah Delectables

All your typical Hanukkah foods are cooked in oil. Fried treats like latkes and donuts have become a tradition because of the miracle in the Hanukkah story, where the one-day supply of oil in the Temple lasted for eight days.

This presents a safety challenge when it comes to preparing these foods in school. It is recommended that students be involved primarily with activities such as mixing ingredients, while leaving the actual cooking and operation of appliances to teachers or to the school's kitchen staff. And if it's possible to have the students present while these foods are frying, even as spectators, it's a good idea to have them stand back far enough to keep them out of risk from contact with the hot oil.

LIP-LICKING LATKES
Ages 8 and up

Potato pancakes, commonly called by their Yiddish name, latkes (they're called *levivot* in Hebrew), are the most popular Hanukkah food. Here's a latke recipe that'll make enough for about eight kids (increase the amount of all ingredients uniformly according to the size of your class). The directions are for the teacher's use, though step 3—mixing all the ingredients in bowls—is fun for the kids as well.

WHAT YOU NEED:

Ingredients
- 6 large potatoes
- 2 eggs
- 1 tsp salt
- ¼ tsp pepper
- 1 large onion
- 3 tbsp flour
- oil
- topping: applesauce and/or sour cream

Utensils
- mixing bowl
- food processor
- measuring spoons
- slotted spatula
- plates
- paper towels
- frying pan

HOW IT'S DONE:

1. Mix the flour, eggs, salt, and pepper in a bowl or food processor.

2. Shred the potatoes and onions separately in the food processor.

3. Mix all ingredients except the oil and toppings until fully mixed.

4. Pour oil into a frying pan, and heat on the stove.

5. Drop large spoonfuls of the potato mixture into the frying pan to form the pancakes. Fry the latkes on both sides until they are golden brown, adding more oil as needed.

6. Drain the latkes on paper towels to absorb the oil.

7. Serve hot with toppings.

APPETIZING APPLESAUCE
Ages 9 and up

Applesauce adds a sweet and refreshing taste to steaming latkes. Here's how to make homemade applesauce. (Note: For classroom purposes, it's recommended that the first three steps are prepared by teacher or kitchen staff before students get involved.)

WHAT YOU NEED:

Ingredients

- 2½ pounds apples
- ⅓ cup apple juice or cider
- 1 tbsp lemon juice
- ground cinnamon
- ground nutmeg (optional)
- honey or brown sugar to taste

Utensils

- paring knife
- cutting board
- heavy saucepan with lid
- measuring cup
- measuring spoons
- wooden spoon or potato masher

HOW IT'S DONE:

1. Peel, core, and quarter the apples, then place them in a heavy saucepan.

2. Add the apple juice. Cover the pot, and bring the liquid to a boil, stirring frequently.

3. Lower the heat to simmer, and cook for another 20 minutes or until the apples are soft. Stir occasionally to be sure the apples don't stick to the bottom. You may need to add more liquid, depending on the type of apples used.

4. Add the lemon juice and ground spices.

5. Mash the apples with a wooden spoon or masher. If desired, add honey or sugar (start with a teaspoon, and add more to taste).

6. Allow the applesauce to cool, and serve it chilled.

7. Spread it on top of your latkes for a great-tasting combination!

FRY 'EM AND TRY 'EM: *SOOFGANIYOT*
Ages 9 and up

Like latkes, *soofganiyot* (donuts or jelly donuts) are another greasy treat traditionally made on Hanukkah, especially in modern-day Israel. Here's a nonjelly recipe, which is a bit easier. For steps 2–8 and 11, get students to help in the preparation; leave the other steps to the adults (teacher or kitchen staff).

WHAT YOU NEED:

Ingredients

- ½ cup butter or margarine
- ¾ cup orange juice
- 6 tbsp sugar
- 2 packages dry yeast
- 4 cups flour
- 2 eggs (beaten)
- 1 tbsp pure vanilla extract
- 2 tsp lemon juice
- oil for frying
- sugar (powdered or regular) or cinnamon for coating
- resealable clear plastic bag

Utensils

- measuring cup
- measuring spoons
- small saucepan
- wooden stirring spoon
- large bowl
- bread board or smooth surface
- bread bowl (greased)
- rolling pin
- butter knife
- frying pan
- slotted spoon

HOW IT'S DONE:

1. Heat the butter (or margarine), orange juice, lemon juice, and sugar in a small saucepan until the butter is melted. Mix well, and transfer the liquid to a large bowl, then allow it to cool for about 5 minutes.

2. Add the yeast, and mix well.

3. Add flour, eggs, and vanilla. Mix with a wooden spoon.

4. On a floured surface and with floured hands, knead the dough for about 10 minutes. Add more flour if the dough is too sticky.

5. Place the dough in a greased bowl, and allow it to rise for about 30 minutes.

6. Punch down the dough, and knead it for about 5 minutes, then cover and let it rise for another 30 minutes.

7. On a floured surface, roll the dough about one inch thick.

8. Cut off small round pieces from the roll, about the size of donut holes.

9. Heat about one inch of oil in a pan until it is hot.

10. Drop in the dough pieces and cook until they are golden, then lift the *soofganiyot* with a spoon and put them on paper towels to drain the oil.

11. Put sugar or cinnamon (or both) in the sealable plastic bag. Once the *soofganiyot* have cooled a little, add several to the bag, seal it, and gently shake until the *soofganiyot* are coated.

12. Serve them up!

6 Tu B'Shvat

Tu B'Shvat is the Jewish Arbor Day or Earth Day. The holiday comes on the fifteenth day of the Hebrew month of Shvat—thus the name Tu (the alphabetic equivalent of the number fifteen) B'Shvat (meaning "in Shvat"). While the holiday falls in January or February—when it's still cold in many parts of the Northern Hemisphere—at that time in Israel the rainy season is ending and the trees have begun to bud.

In the sixteenth century, the kabbalists (followers of Kabbalah, or Jewish mysticism) in the town of Sfat (in the Galilee) started a special tradition for Tu B'Shvat: a communal meal with a set order, similar in format to the Passover seder—complete with four cups of wine. But instead of celebrating freedom from slavery, the Tu B'Shvat seder celebrates the renewal of the trees. While this seder had fallen out of wide practice for many years, it has recently begun to make a comeback with the growing popularity of both Kabbalah and environmentalism. Because Tu B'Shvat is not the type of religious holiday where school is canceled, the classroom provides a perfect place to celebrate the day with a seder.

Today, on Tu B'Shvat, many Jews direct their attention toward the produce in the Land of Israel and reflect on the way they treat nature. It's a great chance to talk with your class about recycling and other everyday ways to help the environment. Also consider inviting others to celebrate Tu B'Shvat with your class—eating fruits associated with Israel, having a Tu B'Shvat seder, and maybe even planting a tree that will endure for many years to come.

"Fruits of Israel"

The foods that we especially try to eat on Tu B'Shvat are tree fruits traditionally associated with the Land of Israel: grapes, figs, pomegranates, olives, dates, almonds, and carob. The first five of these fruits are featured in Deuteronomy 8:8. Almonds are the first fruit trees to blossom at this time of year in Israel. And carob is a non-perishable fruit that grows wild in Israel.

THE "NATURE NOSH" TU B'SHVAT SEDER
Ages 7 and up

Because there are no set rules for the Tu B'Shvat seder, customs will vary, but all Tu B'Shvat practices involve sharing delicious natural foods and drinks with friends. In a classroom environment, the seder can be held instead of an afternoon snack or following lunch.

To set up the seder, have your class decorate their tables with flowers and plants, and provide each student with a clear drinking glass. In addition to the "fruits of Israel," try to serve some fruits that you might not typically eat, and if time and resources permit, consider whipping up fruit smoothies or a fruit salad.

The following is an example of a simple seder you can do with your class. (For information about a school-friendly Tu B'Shvat Haggadah, see page 167.) It involves drinking four cups of grape juice, each one representing a different season, and eating four types of fruit, each symbolizing a season as well as one of the four elements in nature: earth, water, air, and fire. Traditionally, Jews say a prayer of gratitude for each cup of wine and for each type of fruit consumed. For these prayers, see Appendix of Prayers, pages 199–200.

WHAT YOU NEED:

Utensils
- clear (plastic) wine cups for everyone
- plates for everyone
- nutcrackers (optional)

Ingredients
- equal amount of white and red grape juice
- 4 different types of tree fruits or nuts, arranged on serving plates:
    - ✦ fruit with an outer layer that cannot be eaten (such as almond, kiwi, pomegranate)
    - ✦ fruit with an inner core that cannot be eaten (such as date, peach, or plum)
    - ✦ fruit that is completely edible (fig, carob, grape)
    - ✦ edible seeds (such as sunflower seeds and pumpkin seeds)

HOW IT'S DONE:

1. Fill the cups with white grape juice. This symbolizes winter. Drink approximately one quarter of the juice.

2. Eat the foods with a peel or shell that can't be eaten. The peels and shells represent the earth; we eat these nuts and hard-skinned fruits to remind us of the protection the earth provides in the form of shelter and food.

3. For the second drink of juice, refill your cups to the top, using a small amount of red grape juice. This symbolizes spring, when white becomes pink as the new growth appears. Drink about half of the juice in the cup.

4. Eat the fruit that has a tough inner core and a soft outer part. With this fruit we remember that our "inner selves"—our hearts and minds—have to remain strong even when our "outer cores"—our bodies—are not. This fruit also symbolizes water, the second element of nature. Water seems weak but has great power.

5. For the third drink of juice, refill your cups to the top once more with red juice to make the juice even darker in color. This symbolizes summer, when we see bright-colored flowers and the sun shining bright. Again, drink about half of the juice.

6. Eat the fruit that is completely edible. This represents the third element, air, which has no barriers.

7. Refill your cups for a fourth time, again with red grape juice, to turn the color of the juice completely red. It reminds us of the rich colors found at the beginning of autumn.

8. Eat the fourth food, seeds, which represent the final element of nature: fire. This reminds us that fire can be created by a particle as small as a seed.

9. End the seder by enjoying any of the "fruits of Israel" that you have not yet eaten during the seder, as well as any other natural treats you have prepared.

10. While you are noshing (an English word taken from the Yiddish for "snack"), ask the students in the class to suggest ways to do something that is "nature positive," such as recycling more, saving water by turning off the tap while brushing your teeth, or conserving electricity by remembering to turn off the lights when you leave a room.

Hebrew Horticulture

CLASSROOM GARDENING
Ages 6–12

Planting is a great way to celebrate Tu B'Shvat. And kids love gardening: getting dirty, digging, planting something, and watching it grow. What could be more fun?

If, where you live, winter is warm enough to plant outside—well, you're very lucky! Your class can get a jump start on spring by doing some outdoor gardening for Tu B'Shvat in the school or neighborhood garden. But even if it's too cold during January or February for outdoor gardening, that shouldn't stop you from doing a little planting right inside the classroom. Here are some simple ideas:

- *Plant a window garden* Start a window flower garden with seeds or bulbs (available at a garden center). Some of the best bulbs for an indoor pot are tulips, hyacinths, and narcissus. Your class can take these flowers out of their pots and plant them outside in the garden once spring comes. But they'll do well inside with plenty of water and light.

- *Grow baby fruit trees* Collect seeds from apples, oranges, lemons, or other fruit. Rinse them off, and let them soak in water overnight. Then, using good potting soil, plant the seeds in indoor pots. Keep the soil moist, and make sure the plants are getting plenty of light. Within six weeks you should see plants sprouting. If you want to try to get these plants to produce fruit and you live in an appropriate climate, you can transfer them outside once it gets warm out. But they'll make nice plants to keep inside the class, too.

- *Make an avocado sprout* Fill a jar with water. Then take an avocado pit and stick three toothpicks into it so that you can prop the pit at the mouth of the jar, with half of the pit dipping into the water (and the toothpicks holding the other half out of the water). In about a month, the avocado pit will crack open and a little tree will sprout out of it. Once this little tree gets going a bit, you can plant it into a pot of soil or outside. The avocado plant is very pretty and has nice big leaves.

Gardening by Phone or Keyboard

For Jews, tree planting and farming have traditionally been a big deal in the Land of Israel. The process of cultivating our ancient homeland symbolizes our deep roots there. If your class would like to plant a tree in Israel for Tu B'Shvat but can't arrange the very long and expensive field trip over there to do it yourselves, you can contact the Jewish National Fund (JNF) at 800-542-8733 or www.jnf.org. For the cost of a donation, which your class can raise together, the JNF will plant a tree for you. They'll send you a certificate with your name on it.

TURNING PAPER BACK INTO A TREE

Ages 6–10

This craft makes a great table center-piece for your class's Tu B'Shvat seder.

WHAT YOU NEED:

Materials
- paper towel tube
- shoebox lid
- 3 pieces of construction paper (pick colors appropriate for tree leaves)

Equipment
- pencil
- sharp-edged scissors (for teacher)
- paints (and brushes) or markers
- clear plastic tape
- scissors (for child)

HOW IT'S DONE:

1. Lay the box lid on your work surface so that its underside faces up. Stand the paper towel tube atop the middle of the box lid, and trace with a pencil the round bottom of the tube onto the lid.

2. Cut out the circle you traced, to create a hole in the box top, but don't cut any other part of the box lid. (For kids too young to handle sharp scissors, teachers should do this step.)

3. Paint or color the tube and the box lid. (The top of the lid will become the "ground"; its underside will not be visible.)

4. Stick the tube through the hole you cut in the lid.

5. Roll two or three pieces of colored paper together into a tubular shape (small enough to fit it later inside the paper towel tube). Tape one end of the paper in place so it will stay in that shape.

6. At one end of the colored paper tube, cut with your scissors 5 inches deep. Repeat that cut every half-inch (going around the tube) to create frayed strips at that end.

7. Slide the colored paper tube inside the cardboard tube, leaving the strips sticking out of the cardboard. Bend the strips over the edge of the cardboard tube so they look like tree branches.

7 Purim

As you may know, the "funnest" of all Jewish holidays is Purim, celebrated in early spring. The story of Purim, which is told in the Book of Esther (*Megillat Esther,* or "the *Megillah*"), is set in ancient Persia (modern-day Iran). Its two heroes are Esther—a beautiful young Jewish woman—and her uncle Mordecai. Esther marries the king, Ahasuerus, and becomes queen without disclosing that she is Jewish. The villain of the story, Haman, is the king's right-hand man. He gets permission to kill all the Jews in the land until Esther asks the king to spare her people—revealing that she is a Jew. When the king realizes the full import of Haman's evil plans he arranges for the Jews to be saved and orders that Haman be put to death.

Kids (teachers too!) traditionally dress up in costumes on this holiday, and school is a great place for everyone to come in costume and have Purim parties. The real lesson of Purim, though, is that we don't need to disguise ourselves. Although it's easy to blend in, it's also important to remember who we are as Jews.

On Purim, few of the regular "holiday rules" apply—in synagogue, school, or anywhere else. There are carnival-like celebrations, funny skits, and people (including teachers and rabbis) acting generally silly. When the *Megillah* is read (typically in synagogue, but possibly in school as well), everyone listens carefully to the story until the reader comes to the word "Haman," at which point everyone makes a lot of noise to drown out his name. We can boo,

hiss, stamp our feet, and twirl or shake a noise-maker—called a
grogger in Yiddish, *ra'ashan* in Hebrew.

THE "SHAKE-RATTLE-AND-ROLL" *GROGGER*
Ages 3–6

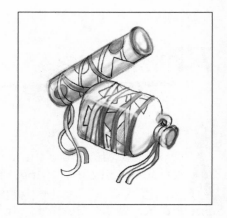

WHAT YOU NEED:

Materials
- metal or plastic container with a lid or cap, such as a tennis ball can or small milk or juice carton
- colored paper, contact paper, stickers, other decorations
- dried beans, seeds, or popcorn kernels

Equipment
- glue
- packing tape

HOW IT'S DONE:

1. Decorate the container's exterior with contact paper, colored paper, or stickers—and allow it to dry if necessary.

2. Fill the container with dried beans, seeds, or popcorn kernels. (These items are choking hazards, so young children should be supervised carefully.)

3. Put the lid or cap on. Tape or glue it shut around the rim or mouth (to prevent accidents). Get ready to shake, rattle, and roll!

The Costume Department

Kids can wear any type of costume on Purim, but it's especially fun to dress up like the characters in the Purim story itself. There are the good guys: Queen Esther and Mordecai. And of course, there's the ultimate bad guy, Haman.

"PURIM PUNIM" FACE PAINTS
Ages 6–12 (paint mixing); all ages (providing faces to paint on)

Here's a quick and easy way to create a set of six different-colored paints. They're safe for use on cute little faces, for Purim or whenever!

WHAT YOU NEED:
Ingredients
- 6 tsp cornstarch
- 3 tsp water
- 3 tsp cold cream
- food coloring

Utensils
- muffin tin with 6 cups
- measuring spoons
- paintbrushes (the smaller the better)

HOW IT'S DONE:

1. In each cup of the muffin tin, put 1 tsp of cornstarch, 1/2 tsp of cold cream and 1/2 tsp of water.

2. Add different colors of food coloring to each cup, mixing some colors to create more options.

3. Mix well.

4. Have teachers or students over 8 paint decorations on faces. Do a small design on foreheads or cheeks, or if there's enough paint, color an entire face.

CROWNS FIT FOR A KING OR QUEEN
Ages 5–10

The following is one possibility for making a homemade crown. Kids can also decorate their crowns with markers, sequins, or rhinestones. For younger kids who can't use scissors safely, consider having the crown shapes already cut out for them before beginning.

WHAT YOU NEED:

Materials
- large paper or posterboard
- glitter glue or markers, rhinestones, sequins
- white glue

Equipment
- pencil
- scissors
- stapler

HOW IT'S DONE:

1. Provide each student with a large piece of paper or posterboard and have them wrap it around their head to figure out the size of their crown. Mark the length with a pencil, allowing a little extra overlap room to fasten the ends together.

2. Cut the paper or posterboard to size.

3. Have students figure out how tall they want their crowns to be, and then trim the paper or posterboard using a zig-zag pattern to form the points of the crowns. (Draw guidelines on the paper first if that helps.)

4. Lay the cut paper or posterboard out flat.

5. Decorate the outside of the crown, using glitter glue or markers, rhinestones, and sequins. (Young children might do better with markers than with glitter glue.) Let your crown dry completely.

6. Have students wrap the paper around their heads again to confirm the exact size the crowns should be. They should hold that size in place as they remove the crown from their head.

7. Staple the crown so that it remains circular and fits on their heads.

8. Wear it like a king or queen!

An even easier method for making crowns is to take premade ones (like the ones you can get from Burger King) and then paint or decorate them as you please.

THREE POINTS: A HAMAN HAT TRICK
Ages 6–12

The villain Haman is said to have worn a triangular black hat. No Haman costume is complete without one. Here's how kids can make their own, perhaps as an alternative to making the crown:

WHAT YOU NEED:
Materials
- black construction paper

Equipment
- ruler
- scissors
- pencil
- measuring tape
- clear plastic tape

HOW IT'S DONE:

1. From thick construction paper, cut out a circle that's 12 inches in diameter. (Teachers may want to create a circle stencil and have students trace it onto the construction paper before cutting.)

2. In the center of that circle, cut a smaller circle that's as big as the child's head (measure first to ensure it will be just snug enough to stay above the child's ears.)

3. With a pencil and ruler, lightly draw a triangle on the paper, around the cut-out circle, out to the edges of the paper.

4. Fold the edges up along the triangle's lines, to form the three-cornered hat.

5. Tape the edges in place at the inside corners, and there you have it: one "mean" Haman hat!

The *Purim-Shpiel* Must Go On!

Now that your students are all dressed up, let's give them someplace to go! The costumes they make will come in handy, since it's traditional on Purim to put on a play that tells the story of this holiday. In Yiddish it's called a *Purim-shpiel*.

Kids often know the story well enough by an early age that little preparation or script is needed to put on the play in class. Consider dividing the class into smaller groups to present parts of the Purim story to the rest of the class. Or if you want to go all-out, have your students stage a full-blown production and invite parents to a daytime or evening performance.

For a smaller-scale production, kids can put on a puppet show to tell the Purim story. And if they need some help telling the story, ready-made *Purim-shpiel* scripts are available in books or on the Web (see *The Whole Megillah (Almost)* from Kar-Ben in the books section on page 167–168; or go to www.akhlah.com/holidays/purim/purim_play.asp).

WHAT A "CAST" OF CHARACTERS: PAPIER-MÂCHÉ PUPPETS
Ages 9–13

Using puppets, kids can perform a whole *Purim-shpiel* with only one or two people. Puppets made from papier-mâché—a soft material that can be molded but then hardens like a plaster cast—are fun and easy to make. But the process takes a few days, so plan ahead. Here's how to do it.

WHAT YOU NEED:

Materials
- dry laundry starch, or glue
- cold water
- newspaper
- balloons
- cardboard toilet-paper rolls (empty)
- acrylic paints
- cloth, yarn, glue (optional)

Equipment
- mixing bowl
- whisk
- paintbrushes

HOW IT'S DONE:

1. Mix the starch (or glue) and water in equal amounts. Whisk until fully blended, then allow it to stand and thicken.

2. Tear newspaper into strips. (Newspaper tears easily from top to bottom.) Dip these strips into the mixture so they become saturated with the white concoction to make the papier-mâché.

3. Blow up a balloon to roughly the size you would like your puppet's head to be. Let the balloon rest on top of a cardboard toilet-paper roll. This cardboard tube will become the handle for the puppet.

4. Wrap the papier-mâché around the balloon and the cardboard handle, shaping it to create the head of the character. Shape ears, nose, eyes, mouth, and hair (or you can paint these on later, after the head has dried).

5. Let it dry for about three days, depending on the thickness, until the head becomes completely hard.

6. Once it is dry, use acrylic paints to add color to the faces of the Purim characters. You can also glue on hair or clothes using cloth or yarn. Or you can make one of the hats described above for your puppet to wear.

7. It's show time!

THE "SO-GOOD-YOU'LL-EAT-YOUR-HAT" HAMANTASCHEN

Ages 5–12

Hamantaschen are the traditional Purim treat. They are triangular-shaped cookies, said to look like Haman's hat. Use whatever kind of filling you like (we've made a few suggestions in this recipe). We guarantee they'll be delicious, or we'll eat our hat—as long as it's Haman's!

WHAT YOU NEED:

Ingredients

- 2 cups flour (plus extra for flouring the surfaces)
- ½ cup sugar
- 1½ tsp baking powder
- ½ tsp salt
- 2 eggs
- ½ cup margarine or butter
- 1 tsp vanilla
- suggested fillings:

    + preserves or jams (apricot or raspberry are best)

    + poppy seed filling (store bought)

    + chocolate chips
- oil (for greasing the cookie sheet)

Utensils

- large mixing bowl
- measuring cup
- measuring spoons
- stirring spoon or food processor
- bread board
- rolling pin
- cookie cutter (or drinking glass)
- finger bowl with water
- spoon
- cookie sheet

HOW IT'S DONE:

1. Mix first seven ingredients in a large bowl. Blend well by hand until a stiff ball of dough is formed (add a little more flour if it is very soft).

2. Wrap the dough in plastic, put in the refrigerator, and allow to chill overnight.

3. Divide the dough in half.

4. Roll out one half of the dough until it is about ¼ inch thick. Then, using a cookie cutter (or the rim of a cup), cut circles about 3 inches in diameter in the dough. (Lift away the excess dough, and roll it out again until there is not enough to cut out circles.)

5. Dip your finger in water and run it around the edge of the dough circles you cut.

6. Spoon the filling of your choice into the center of the circle—about one scant teaspoon per circle.

7. Fold the sides of the circle up, on top of the filling, three times, to turn the circle into a triangle. Pinch together the folds of dough where they overlap at the three points of the triangle to ensure that the pocket doesn't spread open.

8. Place the triangles on a greased cookie sheet and bake at 325°F for 12–15 minutes or until they start to brown on the bottom and edges.

Special Delivery: *Mishloach Manot*

While there's a lot of fun to be had during Purim, our good fortune is meant to be shared with others. That's why, in addition to the every-day Jewish value of *tzedakah* (provid-ing for everyone's basic needs), Purim specifically involves giving money to the needy. Another part of Purim's celebration is deliv-ering "care packages" to our friends and family. This is called *mishloach manot.*

These "care packages" can be filled with all sorts of ready-to-eat goodies and little gifts—including hamantaschen—and they're fun to assemble as a class project (ask students to sign up to bring in dif-ferent treats to put in the packages). They can be carried in baskets, paper bags, or even containers that your class has made and deco-rated. Use stickers, ribbons, and markers to make the *mishloach manot* package as beautiful as you can. Then you can send packages home with the students or go and drop off packages in person to other staff or neighbors.

Backwards Day

Purim is the Jewish "Backwards Day." In the Book of Esther, there are many reversals of fortune: Instead of the Jews being massacred, they are honored and their enemies are destroyed. Haman is killed on the same contraption he had built to kill Mordecai, and Mordecai is honored in the same way that Haman had planned for himself to be honored. The story also involves the reversal of roles. For example, the king takes orders from his servants when they give him the idea to put Haman to death.

With that in mind, why not celebrate this holiday as a "Backwards Day" in your class? Expand on traditional observances in the wild spirit of Purim. Have the teachers and students switch roles for a while. Wear your clothes backwards. Have the students assign the teachers homework. Eat lunch backward—dessert first!

8 Passover

Passover, or *Pesach* in Hebrew, is a springtime holiday that cele-brates freedom. We remember that our ancestors were slaves in Egypt and retell the story of the Exodus—how they were set free.

For older classes, consider discussing with students the things that "enslave" us today. Is it pressure to succeed at school or in sports? Perhaps something else? Striving for excellence is impor-tant, but when are kids getting too much pressure (from others or themselves) to "do it all"? Passover is a time to concentrate on free-ing ourselves from that which enslaves us and to appreciate the freedom we have.

Passover Prep Work

OPERATION FEATHER-AND-CANDLE
Ages 3–8

Among the many customs associated with Passover, one of the best known is the practice of eating only unleavened bread (made from dough that has not risen). All the food that is made from leavened bread is considered *chametz,* not kosher for Passover. We clean our houses of all the *chametz* on the days before the holiday starts. We can also clean our classrooms in preparation for Passover.

After we've done a thorough "spring cleaning," we do one final search for any *chametz* we may have missed the first time around. It's easy to make this tradition a fun activity in class and make kids feel like they're part of an important—and highly delicate—mission.

The custom (going back to the days before the Dustbuster and flashlight) is to carry a candle, a feather, and a wooden spoon on this hunt for *chametz*. You use the feather to sweep the food into the wooden spoon. The candle is used for light, since the search is traditionally done on the night before Passover begins (if you're doing it in class during the day, just turn off the overhead lights to create the illusion of nighttime).

Teachers can carry the candle (or better yet, use a flashlight to be safe); students can carry the feather and wooden spoon. Have a paper bag handy so you can put all the *chametz* in it and dispose of it properly.

Note to teachers: To make sure the search is successful, it's customary to hide a few wrapped pieces of bread or crackers (classic *chametz* culprits) around the room beforehand. Or, put wrapped pieces of candy around the room; when the kids find it, they'll have a final *chametz* snack before Passover begins.

UNDERCOVER MATZAH

Ages 4–10

Matzah is the flat—that is, unleavened—bread that the Israelites brought with them when they were rushing out of Egypt, when they had no time to wait for the bread to rise. By eating matzah on Passover, we celebrate freedom.

On the Passover seder table, we stack three pieces of matzah to use for display and for ceremonial eating. (Also, the middle matzah in the stack will be broken in two and half of it set aside as the *afikomen*—see page 70). And of course, there's plenty more matzah that's just for regular eating with dinner.

Here's an easy way for your students to make a matzah cover with three pockets to use for the three pieces of matzah on their family seder tables.

WHAT YOU NEED:

Materials

- 4 square pieces of felt or fabric, bigger than a piece of matzah (you can buy precut squares at a craft store)
- bottles of fabric paint
- glue
- decorations: sequins, buttons, rhinestones

Equipment

- stapler (for teachers' use with younger kids)

HOW IT'S DONE:

1. Stack the four pieces of felt on top of one another.

2. Around three sides of the stack, staple the pieces together to create a pouch with three pockets—one for each of the three pieces of matzah. Line the staples about a half inch from the edge of the felt pieces.

3. Fold and glue the edges of the bottom and top pieces of felt over the exposed top and bottom of the staples so that you can no longer see the staples.

4. Decorate the top piece of felt (students can do this before or after they've attached the pieces) using fabric paint. Write "Matzah" in English or Hebrew in the center of the cover (see Appendix of Stencils, page 208).

5. Glue on sequins, buttons, and rhinestones for a finishing touch.

The Wide World of *Charoset*

The most delicious item found on the seder plate is called *charoset*. It's a fruit-and-nut mixture that looks like cement or mud. It represents the mortar that the Israelite slaves used when building the Egyptian cities for Pharaoh.

Here are two different recipes for *charoset*, taken from two different parts of the world. Both serve twenty to twenty-five people. Have the students help by measuring and mixing the ingredients, while teachers do the cutting and operate the food processor.

A TRADITIONAL
ASHKENAZI *CHAROSET*
Ages 5 and up

WHAT YOU NEED:

Ingredients
- 6 large apples, peeled and cored
- 2 cups crushed walnuts
- 2½ tsp cinnamon
- 3½ ounces honey
- 1 cup sweet red wine or red
  grape juice

Utensils
- food processor
- measuring cup
- measuring spoons

HOW IT'S DONE:

Blend all the ingredients in a food processor until almost smooth.
Refrigerate.

FARID'S PERSIAN VERSION *CHAROSET*

WHAT YOU NEED:

Ingredients
- 2 cups shelled pistachio nuts
- 1 cup shelled pecans
- 1 cup shelled walnuts
- 2 cups shelled filbert nuts
- 2 medium-size apples, peeled
  and sliced
- 2 medium-size pears, peeled
  and sliced
- 2 cups raisins
- 1 cup pitted dates
- 2 tsp cinnamon
- ½ tsp ginger
- ½ cup sweet red wine or red
  grape juice

Utensils
- food processor
- measuring cup
- measuring spoons
- mixing bowl
- mixing spoon

HOW IT'S DONE:

1. Chop all the nuts in the food processor, and place them in a large bowl.

2. Chop the apples and pears together in the food processor.

3. Add the raisins and dates to the apple and pear mixture, and process again.

4. Combine all the ingredients in the bowl.

5. Add cinnamon, ginger, and juice and mix thoroughly, kneading by hand. Refrigerate.

Note: Leftover *charoset* stays good in the refrigerator for several weeks. Both at the seder and later, it's a good idea to add a bit of grape juice to moisten the *charoset*. Mix it in just before serving.

The Interactive Model Seder

We have seders each year to pass down from generation to generation the story of the Exodus. While the real seders take place in our homes at night, many schools hold model seders to teach students about the customs and to allow them to take a leadership role in the meal.

The Haggadah is the guidebook that takes us through the seder. There are many *Haggadot* (plural of Haggadah) out there, with a variety of different styles to choose from. Take the time to look at a few and pick out the one that feels most comfortable for use in a classroom situation. Familiarize yourself with the Haggadah before your model seder; decide ahead of time which parts you're going to do, which parts you'll skip, and what discussions and activities you'll add to personalize the seder for your class. Here are some ideas to make your model seder fun and meaningful.

CHARTING THE SEDER COURSE
Ages 6–12

With a Haggadah as a guide, your students can make charts that list all the parts of the Passover seder. Placing this simple prop on their seder tables is a great way to keep kids tuned in and involved with what's happening. During your seder, they can follow along and keep track of how far they've gotten in the seder and how much is left. They'll like putting stickers next to all the parts that have been completed, and they'll look forward to all the parts coming up. And afterward, the kids can take their charts home to use in their family seders.

WHAT YOU NEED:

Materials
- construction paper
- clear contact paper
- stickers

Equipment
- markers
- scissors

HOW IT'S DONE:

1. On the construction paper, make a chart with the order of the seder, listing the Hebrew or English words for each part of the seder. Use the fourteen-item list in your Haggadah.

2. Draw pictures for the different parts, such as a Kiddush cup for the Kiddush and matzah for the ceremonial eating of the matzah.

3. Laminate the paper with clear contact paper to make it a place mat for the seder. Trim with scissors.

4. Give out stickers to the students. As you finish each part of the seder, they can use a sticker to mark the part you've just completed.

Enough Food to Go Around

During the seder, we say, "Let all who are hungry come eat, let all who are needy come to our Passover feast." Since we don't really expect those who are hungry to just walk in, try this to give real meaning to those words: Ask students to bring cans of food to the seder that you'll donate to a local soup kitchen. Also, make an effort to invite some guests who might not otherwise experience a Passover seder.

Dress Up and Lie Down

Instead of doing the seder while seated at a long table, as is usually the custom, consider having your class sit on a carpet or blanket on the floor with pillows or cushions for comfort. This is a great way to take away any "stuffy atmosphere" that may come with a formal table setting and to make the whole event more fun and cozy. Also, it allows us to have our seder in a truly "reclining" position, as the Haggadah says we should, to show that we are free—and to make this "night" different from all other "nights."

Have your class dress up in comfortable Israelite/Egyptian garb for the seder. Participants can take off their shoes. Decorate the classroom like a tent by stringing up sheets or tapestries. Kids really get into this, and it sets the right kind of mood for a truly "Interactive Model Seder." It lets everyone know, right off the bat, that this is not going to be "seder-as-usual." And since we are supposed to retell the Passover story as if it happened to us personally, dressing up helps fuel the kids' imaginations.

Encourage your class to "feel comfortable"—encourage students or guests to ask questions throughout the seder. Questions are an important part of this holiday, because questions push us all to think, share ideas, and come up with answers. With new questions and new discussions every year, no two seders are ever exactly alike. Strive to retell the story of the Exodus in a way that is fresh and relevant to the lives of your students today.

Middle Matzah Mania

Once the *afikomen* is broken off from the middle matzah and wrapped in a cloth napkin, some seders follow an old custom where the leader takes the *afikomen* and puts it on his or her shoulder, as if it were a sack of food being carried out of Egypt by the Israelites. The leader takes a few steps and says, "This is in memory of our ancestors, who left Egypt carrying the bread of affliction on their shoulders." Visual images like this make it easier for kids to follow the story.

Sometimes the leader of the seder asks a child to march with the *afikomen* on his or her shoulder (several students can take turns). The leader asks the child, "Where are you going?" And the child responds, "Out of Egypt." Then the leader says, "And what are you carrying on your shoulder?" And the child answers, "The matzah, the bread that didn't have a chance to rise before our journey."

Of course, there's more fun in store with the *afikomen*. Perhaps the seder tradition most popular with kids is hiding this piece of matzah. After the meal, the seder cannot resume (and conclude) until the *afikomen* has been found. But who hides it? And then who finds it? Well, there are many variations on this tradition. But for the most part, they fall into two categories:

- The leader of the seder hides the *afikomen* at some point when the kids are not watching. The children search for it, and there's usually a reward for the child who finds it.

- In another tradition, the kids sneak off with the *afikomen* and hide it from the leader of the seder, who has to pay a "ransom" to get it back.

Of course, a model seder with a class full of kids presents special challenges. If the group is small enough, you may be able to hide the *afikomen* in the classroom without the entire class seeing. If it's not safe and feasible to have the entire class search for it, consider some other simple game (guessing a number or trivia questions, for instance) to determine who wins the reward.

Interactive Israelites

The seder is all about teaching the Passover story to the next generation. It's much easier for kids to learn and understand what it's about when you make the seder interactive and fun for them. Rather than simply sitting and reading, act out as much of the Haggadah as possible and include skits and songs in the seder. This will surely make it more memorable.

It's not easy to make up skits or songs right on the spot, so ask your students to prepare something ahead of time. Assign a different part of the seder to each child or team of kids. Parts of the seder to assign include the Four Questions (how about thinking up "Four More Questions"), the Four Sons (do a skit with them), or the Ten Plagues (make a list of the "Top Ten Rejected Plagues"). It's okay if some parts are done by more than one team, because each will approach it in a different way. Make sure your students understand that their assignment doesn't need to be too elaborate. Tell them to simply have fun with it!

A "Dayenu" You Won't Be Able to Get Enough Of!

The song "Dayenu" (meaning in Hebrew "enough for us") has a fun traditional melody and repetition to it, but there's a way to make it even more exciting. Persian Jews have a custom of playfully hitting each other with scallions during the chorus of this song. Some say we are remembering the whips of the taskmasters, which the scallions resemble, when we do this. Others say we're being playful with the meaning of the song, since people are hitting us with scallions while we're singing, "Enough! Enough!" Either way, as long as you make sure no one gets too rough, it can be fun to give students a chance to give their classmates a playful smack with one of those long green onions!

Open Up! It's Elijah!

At the right point during the model seder, you can ask an unsuspecting student to go open the classroom door to let in the prophet Elijah, as is the custom at seders. The trick is: Without the kids knowing, have an adult (a fellow teacher, parent, or administrator) dress up as Elijah and be waiting outside the door when it's opened. As "Elijah" dramatically enters, it's always funny to see the look of surprise on everyone's faces.

For a fun competition, to keep track of the forty-nine days between the start of Passover and the holiday of Shavuot (these forty-nine days are called the *omer* period), see the Lag B'Omer section, on page 80.

9 Yom Ha'Atzmaut (with Yom Ha'Shoah and Yom Ha'Zikaron)

Yom Ha'Atzmaut is Israeli Independence Day, similar to the American Fourth of July. This holiday celebrates the day—May 14, 1948—when Israel became its own country and the Jewish people gained their national independence for the first time in nearly two thousand years. Because the holiday is celebrated according to the Jewish calendar, it rarely coincides exactly with May 14, but rather falls on a different date each year in late April or early May.

Yom Ha'Atzmaut is a national holiday for Israelis, rather than a religious holiday. It is also observed by many Jews around the world. It has developed into a festival like Purim or Hanukkah, celebrating an against-the-odds victory for the Jewish people.

As is Jewish custom, though, we do not enjoy our victory without acknowledging loss; there can be no good without bad. Therefore, on the day before Yom Ha'Atzmaut we remember all the soldiers who have lost their lives in the struggle to create and protect Israel. This day is called Yom Ha'Zikaron, or "Remembrance Day." At the end of this sad day, a siren sounds all over Israel so that the entire nation remembers the fallen soldiers one more time. When the sirens end, Yom Ha'Zikaron ends and Yom Ha'Atzmaut begins. Celebrations erupt all over the country, with fireworks, music, and dancing in the streets.

One week before Yom Ha'Zikaron and Yom Ha'Atzmaut is another sad day called Yom Ha'Shoah, Holocaust Remembrance Day. On this day, a siren also sounds across Israel, and the entire country comes to a halt. Everyone stops whatever they are doing for a couple of minutes to remember the victims of the Holocaust. People even stop their cars and get out. In America and other countries, people also commemorate those lost in the Holocaust with special services and programs at synagogues, Jewish community centers, and Holocaust memorials.

These three important days offer a good time to take pride in the existence of Israel and also to discuss the events that led to the creation of Israel and the difficulties the country still faces. To celebrate Yom Ha'Atzmaut we can eat Israeli foods, listen to Israeli music, do Israeli dancing (see Jewish Music & Dance, pages 146–150), and make crafts. It's also fun on this day to encourage your class to dress up in blue and white, the colors of the Israeli flag. And your students can also make their own Israeli flag (see page 33 for the flag-making directions in the Simchat Torah section, but paint your flag to look like Israel's flag with two horizontal blue stripes and a solid blue Star of David in the center).

Israeli Food Is-really Good

Many of the foods that we commonly recognize as Israeli are actually Israeli versions of generic Middle Eastern foods. These treats are also enjoyed by people in Israel's neighboring Arab countries. By eating these foods in celebration of Israeli independence, we also recognize that Jews and Arabs are ancient cousins with many things in common culturally.

THE "STUFF-IT-'TIL-IT-STUFFS-YOU" FALAFEL
Ages 10 and up

Having falafel for lunch in Israel is as common as having a burger in America. Falafel are balls of deep-fried ground chickpeas mixed with yummy spices. They're usually served in a pita pocket with hummus and Israeli salad (see recipes below), tahini (sesame) sauce, and other goodies—even french fries. It's a vegetarian delight, though with all this deep-frying, you can be sure it's not health food!

Note: Many of the steps in this recipe are not appropriate for younger kids, so we suggest you limit student participation to steps involving mixing ingredients and shaping the falafel balls before frying.

WHAT YOU NEED:

Ingredients

- 1 16-ounce can chickpeas (drained)
- 1 large onion, chopped
- 7 tbsp finely chopped parsley
- 1 egg, lightly beaten
- 1 tsp salt
- ½ tsp ground hot red pepper (for spicy, 1 tsp)
- 1 tsp garlic powder
- ½ tsp ground cumin (for spicy, 1 tsp)
- ½ to 1 cup bread crumbs
- vegetable oil

Utensils

- can opener
- knife and cutting board
- small bowl or cup
- fork (to beat the egg)
- mixing bowl
- mixing spoon
- measuring spoons
- blender
- frying pan
- slotted spoon
- paper towels or brown paper bags

HOW IT'S DONE:

1. Mix the chickpeas and the onion. Add the parsley, egg, salt, and spices.

2. Whirl the ingredients in a blender, adding bread crumbs until the chickpea mixture is firm enough to form small balls that won't stick to your hands.

3. Form the mix into balls about the size of a quarter (or larger), and flatten them slightly.

4. Fry them in one-inch-deep hot oil until they are golden brown on each side. (Teacher or kitchen staff only.)

5. Remove the falafel from the oil with a slotted spoon, and drain the balls on a paper towel or brown paper bags.

6. Allow them to cool off slightly before making your falafel pita.

ALIZA'S SPREADABLE EDIBLE INCREDIBLE HUMMUS

Ages 8 and up

Like falafel, hummus is made from chickpeas. But instead of being fried, the chickpeas are mashed into a delicious smooth spread that is then either added to a falafel pita or eaten as a dip. Here's how to make it.

WHAT YOU NEED:

Ingredients
- 2 cups canned chickpeas
- 1 cup tahini (sesame) paste (found in most health food stores and kosher markets)
- ¾ cup lemon juice
- 4 garlic cloves, minced
- ½ tsp salt
- ½ tsp cumin
- olive oil, chopped parsley, paprika (optional)

Utensils
- measuring cup
- measuring spoons
- food processor or blender (for use by teacher or kitchen staff)

HOW IT'S DONE:

1. Place all the ingredients (except olive oil, parsley, and paprika) in a food processor or blender. Mix until the chickpeas are smooth.

2. Store the hummus in a covered container in the refrigerator.

3. Serve cold or at room temperature. Just before serving, pour on 1 tbsp of olive oil and sprinkle chopped parsley and/or paprika on top.

4. If desired, reserve ¼ cup of unmashed chickpeas to sprinkle on top or mix in with the spread to make "chunky" hummus.

SLICE 'N' DICE ISRAELI SALAD

Ages 10 and up

The vegetables in Israeli salad are cut small so they fit easily into a falafel pita. But this salad is also delicious when eaten alone. Here's how to make it.

WHAT YOU NEED:

Ingredients
- 2 big tomatoes
- 2 cucumbers
- ¼ onion (or 2 scallions)
- 2 tbsp chopped parsley
- olive oil, to taste
- lemon juice, to taste
- salt and pepper

Utensils
- measuring spoons
- mixing bowl
- stirring spoon

HOW IT'S DONE:

1. Dice the tomatoes, cucumbers, and onions in small pieces. (Depending on the age of the students, it might be safer to have this step prepared by teachers or kitchen staff beforehand.)

2. Mix the vegetables in a medium-size bowl.

3. Add the chopped parsley, olive oil, lemon juice, salt, and pepper. (Start with a small amount of each, and season to taste.) Mix it all up.

4. Refrigerate the salad until ready to eat.

"JEW"ELRY
Ages 5–9

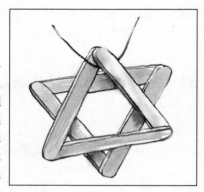

The Star of David is not only a symbol for the Jewish people as a whole, it is also a national symbol of Israel found on the Israeli flag. Here's a "sharp" fashion accessory that can be worn by a girl or a boy on Yom Ha'Atzmaut, whether marching in an official Independence Day celebration or simply showing Israeli pride.

WHAT YOU NEED:

Materials
- 6 Popsicle sticks per necklace
- string
- glitter glue, beads, sequins (optional)

Equipment
- glue
- tempera or acrylic paint

HOW IT'S DONE:

1. Make a triangle out of three of the Popsicle sticks, with the ends overlapping, and glue them together.

2. Form a second triangle with the other three sticks.

3. Glue one triangle on top of the other to form a Jewish star.

4. Decorate the star with paint, glitter glue, beads, or sequins.

5. Allow the star to dry, then put a string through the top point to make a necklace.

10 Lag B'Omer

L ag B'Omer is not among the best-known or most important Jewish holidays, but it's a holiday with plenty of opportunities for fun. The name Lag B'Omer means "the thirty-third day of the *omer*": Lag is a combination of the Hebrew letters *lamed* and *gimmel*, whose numerical values are thirty and three; and the *omer* is the period of forty-nine days between the start of Passover and Shavuot.

The *omer* is considered a sort of mourning period for the twenty-four thousand students of Rabbi Akiba said to have been wiped out in a plague nearly two thousand years ago. Traditionally, Jews don't have weddings, get haircuts, or throw large celebrations during the *omer*. But on the thirty-third day of the *omer*, these restrictions are lifted.

Why the reprieve on Lag B'Omer? According to the Talmud, the plague left students dying in droves on each day of the *omer*. But on the thirty-third day, the plague somehow stopped for just one day.

Burning Bright and Shining Light

One favorite way that Jews around the world celebrate Lag B'Omer is by building bonfires and gathering around to roast marshmallows, sing songs, and tell stories. The bonfires relate to a second historical event connected with Lag B'Omer. It is said that on this day, the great Jewish mystic Rabbi Shimon Bar Yochai (the kabbalistic work of the *Zohar* is often attributed to him) revealed the secrets of the Torah while an "intense light" emanated from his body.

Since having a bonfire means being outdoors, Lag B'Omer is also associated with fun activities such as grilling on the barbecue, having a picnic, or going on a hike. It's a great day for a school-wide outdoor party or even just a simple outing with your class.

If you spend Lag B'Omer at a park or campground and plan to have a bonfire, be sure to follow all the necessary safety precautions. For some basic guidelines on campfire safety, see www.smokeybear.com. Click on "Only You," then click on "Prevention," and then click on "Fire Safety Tips."

DON'T LAG B'HIND
Ages 8–13

The *omer* begins on the second day of Passover and goes for forty-nine days until the start of Shavuot. There's a prayer we say on each of those forty-nine days, and in that prayer we mark what day we're up to in the counting of the *omer*. Getting your students to remember to count each and every day is the key, because if they forget to do it even just one day, they're technically not allowed to count any of the remaining days of the *omer*. You can turn this daily counting into a competition among your students.

HERE'S HOW:
Everyone in the class has to remember to count each day of the *omer*. Every morning, each student writes the number of the day (for example, "Day 1") and his or her name on a small piece of paper and puts it in a designated jar in the classroom. At the end of each day, you check the jar. Everyone who remembered to count the day gets one point. At the end of the forty-nine days, the student with the most points is dubbed "Count *Omer!*"

Viva *Lag* Difference!

The plague that killed Rabbi Akiba's students was said to have been brought on by their own hateful behavior toward one another: intolerance, jealousy, gossiping, and general lack of respect. So one of the holiday's themes is the importance of respecting fellow Jews. Make this holiday an opportunity to concentrate on what you have in common with other Jews who you might otherwise consider to be very different from you.

You could help organize a Lag B'Omer celebration that brings families together from a variety of different congregations in your community. Or you could help arrange a joint activity or project, like a cleanup day or visiting the sick or elderly.

11 Shavuot

The holiday of Shavuot occurs seven weeks after Passover, usually in late May. It celebrates two things: the giving of the Ten Commandments (and many believe the whole Torah) at Mount Sinai after the Israelites left Egypt and also the first fruits of the harvest in ancient Israel.

Pick-'Em-Yourself Fruits and Vegetables

Shavuot is a great time to take your class to an apple orchard, strawberry field, or vegetable farm to really get into the feel of this harvest holiday. In many parts of the United States, late spring—when Shavuot occurs—is prime season for picking certain kinds of fruit. If you call your state agriculture department or your local farmer's market, or look in the local telephone directory or on the Internet, you can usually find "pick-your-own" farms in your area that are open to the public at this time of year. Call ahead; sometimes the picking season is longer or shorter, depending on the weather.

In the Book of Ruth (which takes place at harvest time and is therefore linked to Shavuot), we learn that when you harvest you're supposed to leave part of your crop for the poor. With that in mind, it's a nice idea to donate a portion (or all) of what your class picks to a homeless shelter. If this is not practical to do (or if the shelter will not accept unsealed or perishable foods), then your class can donate canned goods.

MIDNIGHT READ AND FEED
Ages 13 and up

According to Jewish lore, the Torah was given on Mount Sinai at daybreak, but the Israelites overslept and were not prepared for it, so God had to wake them up! To make up for this, it has become a tradition to stay up the entire night on Shavuot, reading the Torah or other Jewish books.

This can be one night when kids are allowed to stay up as late as they want as long as they're reading something that has to do with Judaism. Some older classes might arrange for sleepovers at school and plan learning activities late into the night. If you plan this, also make sure to provide light, refreshing snacks sometime in the middle of the night. Watermelon is a popular choice.

THE LAND OF CHEESE BLINTZES
Ages 9 and up

On Shavuot, it's customary to eat both dairy and sweet foods, since we are celebrating the harvest of the "land of milk and honey." The most popular holiday food has become cheese blintzes with sweet toppings. That lets you cover all your bases in one great treat.

This recipe makes about 15 blintzes, so increase the ingredients uniformly if you need to make more. If your students are too young to cook with a frying pan, just have them help with making the batter and filling and leave the frying to a teacher or kitchen staff.

WHAT YOU NEED:

For the pancakes
- 2 eggs
- ½ tsp salt
- 1 cup milk
- 1 cup flour
- butter

For the filling
- 1 pound dry cottage cheese or farmer cheese
- 1 egg
- salt and pepper, or sugar (to taste)
- measuring cup

HOW IT'S DONE:

1. Beat eggs with salt until they're fluffy.

2. Stir in the milk and flour to make a smooth batter.

3. Melt a very small amount of butter in a six-inch frying pan.

4. Pour into the pan just enough batter (about 2 tbsp) to make a thin coat that covers the whole bottom of the pan.

5. Tilt the pan from side to side to distribute the batter while cooking for a minute or two, until the edges dry and pull away from the pan.

6. Remove the pancake from the pan, and place on a paper towel to cool. Stack the pancakes after they cool.

7. Repeat until no more batter remains.

8. To make the filling, blend the cottage cheese, egg, salt, and pepper (or sugar) in a blender or with a hand mixer until smooth.

9. Place a heaping teaspoon of filling on the fried (bottom) side of each pancake, and fold the sides of the pancake over the filling. Tuck in the ends to keep the cheese inside.

10. Bake the blintzes at 350°F in an oven until crisp and brown.

11. Serve with jelly or fresh fruit.

A House Blooming with Flowers

There is a Shavuot custom of decorating the home with flowers and
plants, and there's no reason you
can't extend the tradition to include
the classroom as well. We do this not
only because the first fruits of the
harvest were brought on this holiday
but also because of the teaching that
when the Torah was given to the
Jewish people at Mount Sinai, the desert around it bloomed and
sprouted flowers.

PRIZE-WINNING PAPER CUTTING
Ages 7 and up

Another customary Shavuot decoration is the paper-cut design. The folk
art of paper cutting was practiced in
nineteenth-century Poland by people
of many different backgrounds and
religions, including the many Jews
who lived there.

Particularly on Shavuot, paper-cut
designs decorated the windows in the
Jewish shtetls, perhaps because they were an inexpensive way to
beautify a home. Floral decorations and ancient symbols were
used: menorahs, crowns, vines, and flowers. These cutouts were
generally made from white paper and mounted on a contrasting
color backing with a short text included.

Below are some basic instructions to get your class started on
some Shavuot paper cutting. Start with really simple designs. Your
students will learn with experience and become experts in no time.

WHAT YOU NEED:

- white paper
- colored construction paper (larger than the white paper)
- glue
- scissors (and graphic arts knives for teachers or high school age students only)
- pencils
- picture frame (to fit)

HOW IT'S DONE:

1. Fold the white paper in half or in fourths, depending on whether you want the designs to appear two times or four times.

2. Lightly sketch in pencil, on the outside of the folded paper, the designs you want to create. (For more elaborate designs, stencils can be used.) If you are creating a design such as vines, don't let the shapes you make run into one another or it will mess up your design.

3. Carefully cut out the design.

4. Unfold the paper to reveal the entire cutout. On the back of your cutout, put a small amount of glue at the corners and a few other spots.

5. Paste the cutout onto the construction paper, and line it up so that it lies flat against the background. If you want to include some writing, leave space for it at the bottom or top.

6. If you choose to include words, write them in the space you left for it. Write "Happy Shavuot" or "Happy Holiday" *(Chag Sameach)* in English or Hebrew (see Appendix of Stencils, page 209), or anything else you'd like to include.

7. Frame your creation, and hang it up to show everyone.

12 Tu B'Av

I t's the Jewish holiday of love. Tu B'Av celebrates romance and marriage, so some view it as a sort of "Jewish Valentine's Day." These days, the observance of this minor secular holiday includes matchmaking and sending roses. Because it falls in the summer, when class is generally not in session, teachers don't often get the chance to share this fun holiday with students. However, if you are teaching a summer program or working at a camp, Tu B'Av can be a highlight of the holiday-deprived summer months.

Tu B'Av is the fifteenth day of the month of Av (Tu combines the Hebrew letters tet and vav, which have the numeric value of fifteen.) It falls six days after Tisha B'Av (ninth of Av), a far more widely observed day of Jewish mourning and fasting. On Tisha B'Av, we remember the many tragedies in Jewish history that occurred on that date, including the destruction of both the First and Second Temples in Jerusalem.

In contrast, Tu B'Av commemorates historic events that helped to unify the Jewish people, including some that deal specifically with marriage and courtship. For example, a law had been enacted during the time of Moses requiring women who inherited property to marry someone from their own tribe. Once the Jewish people settled in the Land of Israel, it was on Tu B'Av that this law was declared obsolete and annulled. Not only was this a victory for women's rights, but it also helped to unify Israel as a single nation once intermarriage between tribes became more common.

IT TAKES TU B'AV TO TANGO
Ages 5 and up

On this "holiday of love," it was a custom in ancient Israel for young, single women to dress in white clothes and go out dancing in the vineyards. Unmarried men would watch, hoping to find a wife. The women wore clothes they had borrowed from each other so they couldn't be judged according to the quality of their dress (that is, how rich they were).

For a fun Tu B'Av celebration, you can stage your own little dress-up-and-dance party. Have everyone collect a few pieces of white clothing of their own, then put all the clothes into a pile, and have everyone pick something out of the pile to wear.

When everyone's dressed in each other's white clothes—underlying how we're all equal as Jews and that it's what's inside that matters more than the kind of clothes we wear—it's time to start dancing! (For some tips on where to begin, see the Jewish Music & Dance section of this book, pages 129–150.) If you really want to go all-out, pack up the boom box and take the kids out to an orchard or forest meadow for some "dancing in the vineyards."

TO MY LOVE ON TU B'AV
Ages 5–10

One nice way to celebrate this holiday is to write notes (similar to Valentine's Day cards) expressing your feelings to the people you care about. Use generic cards that are blank inside so you'll have room to write a nice message. Or better yet, create your own simple heart-shaped cards.

WHAT YOU NEED:
- construction paper
- pencil
- scissors
- markers, glitter glue, crayons, etc.

HOW IT'S DONE:

1. Fold a piece of construction paper in half.

2. Using the folded edge of the paper as one side of your heart, lightly draw in pencil a heart shape on the paper.

3. Cut out the heart shape with the scissors to create your heart-shaped card.

4. On the front of the card, write "Happy Tu B'Av: The Jewish Holiday of Love" (since people who don't know about this holiday might be wondering why you're sending them a Valentine in the middle of the summer).

5. Draw designs around the words as you like.

6. Write a message on the inside of the card, telling the recipient how much they mean to you.

7. Deliver your cards—by hand, if they're going to people who live in your house or by mail if they're going to someone who lives far away (for directions on how to make your own envelopes, see pages 121–122).

13 Celebrating Secular Holidays in a Jewish Way

M any of the holidays we celebrate as Americans contain ideas and messages that work just fine within a Jewish context or that can have Jewish values tacked onto them. During the week in which the holiday falls, talk with your class about the significance of these days and try to draw a Jewish connection. Make the holiday relevant to our lives not only as Americans but also as Jews.

At the most basic level, it's easy to bring Judaism into our secular holiday celebrations with everyday customs such as saying a blessing to mark a particular day or custom. You don't need challah to say the *ha'motzi* blessing on bread. If you're having a cookout for Memorial Day or the Fourth of July, hot dog buns work just as well!

Martin Luther King Jr. Day (January)

There is a significant historic connection between the histories of African-Americans and Jews. We share memories of being subjected to slavery, prejudice, and persecution. But African-Americans and Jewish Americans also have a lot of positive things in common, such as rich cultural heritages and spiritual religious music.

Celebrate this holiday alongside the African-Americans in your community by honoring Dr. Martin Luther King Jr.'s call for justice, peace, and equality. These values are very much in line with Jewish values of social justice. Talk with your students about Dr. King's importance and what Jewish tradition teaches about freedom and prejudice.

Like Passover, this holiday celebrates freedom. But instead of telling our own story, this is the time to let others tell their story—and our turn to listen.

Memorial Day (May)

As we kick off summer with Memorial Day barbecues or trips to the beach it's nice to take a moment to remember what this holiday is all about. Similar to the Israeli Yom Ha'Zikaron, this day honors United States war veterans, both living and dead.

The Jewish War Veterans of the United States of America (JWV) is the oldest active veterans' service organization in America. It was organized in 1896 by Jewish veterans of the Civil War. The group has a program called "The Care Package Campaign," which sends both useful and thoughtful supplies to American Jewish troops serving around the world, on the holidays or any time. The packages contain cards, gifts, treats, reading material, Judaica, and long-distance calling cards.

For more information on how your class can get involved: Jewish War Veterans of the United States of America, 1811 R Street NW, Washington, D.C. 20009. Phone: 202-265-6280; website: www.jwv.org.

Independence Day (July)

Fireworks, barbecues, and picnics—these are all ways we celebrate the Fourth of July. But what we're really celebrating is freedom and independence. The birth of the United States of America on July 4, 1776, established a nation that has for more than two hundred years held freedom and democracy among its primary values and acted as a beacon for those values around the world.

At the time of the Declaration of Independence, about two thousand Jews were living in the thirteen colonies. Some of them fought and died in the Revolutionary War, while others helped the war effort in other ways. They include:

- Francis Salvador—sometimes referred to as the "Paul Revere of the South"—was the first Jew to die in the Revolutionary War, soon after it began, on July 31, 1776. A year before he died, he was elected to the South Carolina state legislature, becoming the first Jew elected to a legislature in the United States.

- Haym Solomon, a Jewish businessman, is largely credited with financing the American Revolution. He raised money to pay for soldiers' clothes, housing, and food.

These individuals fought to create a country where people would be free regardless of religion or class. Today, the United States is truly a dynamic nation made up of diverse people, thanks in part to their efforts. Use the days leading up to July 4th to explore with your class the topics of freedom, diversity, and the values that are both Jewish and American.

Labor Day (September)

It has become a "last fling of summer" celebration, but Labor Day started as a celebration of workers by the labor unions. In 1884, on the first Monday in September, the Knights of Labor organization held a big parade in New York City to honor the working class.

They decided to make it an annual event and named it "Labor Day." The Socialist Party held a similar celebration on May 1, known as May Day, which has since become an international holiday for workers.

In 1894 the U.S. Congress passed a law recognizing Labor Day as an official national holiday. Today, Labor Day is observed not only in the United States but also in Canada and other countries.

Many Jewish immigrants were active in the workers rights and socialist (worker-oriented) movements in New York City from the time they arrived as immigrants through the 1940s. They were in groups like the Arbeiter Ring (which means "Workmen's Circle" in Yiddish) and took leading roles in important unions such as the ILGWU (International Ladies' Garment Workers' Union). Groups like these worked to ensure that the needs, rights, and safety of working people would be respected by large companies.

There's a good chance the grandparents or great-grandparents of your students were somehow involved in or touched by the workers' movement. Encourage the students to ask their families about it, and talk to them about why labor unions were so important at that time. Maybe you could even learn some Yiddish folk songs about unions and workers. Talk with your class about the fairness of labor practices and working conditions today, both in the United States and abroad. Where unfairness exists, discuss how you each can make a difference.

Columbus Day (October)

Columbus Day is celebrated on the second Monday in October to commemorate Christopher Columbus' first landing in North America, on October 12, 1492. He had set sail a few months earlier on an expedition sponsored by Spain.

At that very same time in Spain, Jews were having an extremely difficult time. For hundreds of years previously, Spanish Christians, Muslims, and Jews had coexisted in relative harmony. But in the late 1400s, the Spanish monarchs began an Inquisition, overseen by the pope, to enforce Christianity. The year of Columbus' first voyage, 1492, all the Jews who refused to convert to Christianity were expelled from the country.

Because of what was going on in Spain at the time, there are theories that suggest Columbus himself was Jewish and the expedition was partially supported by Jews in search of a refuge. It is almost certainly true that secret Jews were among Columbus' crew members, including Luis de Torres, a close aide and translator to Columbus who was well versed in Hebrew.

Columbus Day offers a wide range of issues for Jewish classrooms to discuss. You can talk about the value of discovery and perhaps even go for a hike or trip to a place you've never been before (pretend to be explorers!). When thinking about Columbus' interactions with the Native Americans, you can discuss the importance of respecting the property and cultures of others and learn about the connections between Jews and American Indians. (See the book *Jewish Heroes of the Wild West*, listed in our book section on page 153.) With older kids, it's a good time to discuss the Inquisition and the importance of sticking to your beliefs.

Thanksgiving (November)

Thanksgiving is very compatible with Jewish values. As you prepare to spend a day feasting with family, encourage your students to give thanks for all they have. If you have a pre-Thanksgiving program or lunch at school, go around the table and encourage everyone to say one thing for which they're thankful (or just do it during class). You could also have the children draw pictures of those things.

Since the holiday commemorates the feast that newly arrived English settlers shared with Native Americans, encourage students to find out about their own family's immigrant past and report back to the class. You could have a class activity discussing Jewish experiences arriving in this country and how Jews adjusted to their new land. Note that by coincidence, a form of the Hebrew word for "thanks" is also used as the Hebrew word for "turkey," both pronounced "ho-doo."

A great way to show thanks is to give back some of what you have to help others. Encourage students to donate food and money to a soup kitchen or spend part of the week before Thanksgiving helping out there. (Many soup kitchens will be preparing Thanksgiving dinners for the needy.)

Part II
Classroom Fun
for Anytime

14 Volunteerism: *Mitzvot* & *Tzedakah*

nyone who's ever done volunteer work knows it not only makes others feel good but makes you feel good, too. Volunteerism can be a fun and fulfilling experience for everyone involved. Not only that, the act of doing good deeds—sometimes called *tikkun olam* (repairing the world) or *gemilut chasadim* (acts of loving-kindness)—is a cornerstone of Jewish life.

Another Hebrew term used for good deed is *mitzvah*. The more basic meaning of the word, though, is "commandment." Among the 613 commandments for Jews in the Torah are many good deeds. For instance, there's a commandment to "feed the hungry and clothe the naked," which you can do by volunteering at a soup kitchen or by donating clothes to the needy. And there's a commandment to "honor the elderly," which you can do by visiting a retirement home.

Another commandment is *tzedakah*. We often use this word to mean "charity," but it actually means "righteousness." *Tzedakah* is not just about giving; it's also about recognizing what others actually need. Some may need money, while others may need your time and attention. *Tzedakah* should be well thought out. According to the medieval Jewish scholar Maimonides, the best kind of *tzedakah* helps others to help themselves. As the saying goes: "Give people a fish; they eat for a day. Teach them how to fish; they eat for a lifetime."

There are countless ways for your class to perform *mitzvot* (the plural of *mitzvah*) in your school and community. In the coming pages, we'll give you some ideas for projects that are helpful, rewarding, and potentially a lot of fun.

Tzedakah in the Classroom

It's often said that "charity begins at home," but there's no reason it shouldn't continue at school! Either way, it means helping the people who are closest to you. You can begin community-wide activism right in the classroom. Here are some ways to go about doing that.

MAKE YOUR OWN *TZEDAKAH* BOX
Ages 4 and up

A *tzedakah* box is a container that holds the money you set aside for charity. Any container will do just fine—even the most dilapidated box can hold funds that will be extremely helpful and valuable to someone else. Still, it's nice to decorate a *tzedakah* box. And if having a fun-looking *tzedakah* box helps draw people's eyes to it, donations may come in even quicker!

WHAT YOU NEED:
Materials
- old magazines with lots of pictures
- container with removable plastic lid (tennis ball can, coffee tin, etc.)
- clear contact paper (optional)

Equipment
- glue stick
- scissors (and graphic arts knife for teachers only)

HOW IT'S DONE:

1. Cut out magazine pictures of *tzedakah*-related items: food, clothing, people, or words that seem to fit with this theme.

2. Glue the pieces of paper onto the container until it is completely covered.

3. Once the glue has dried, cut a slit in the plastic lid that is large enough to allow a quarter to drop in.

4. If you want, you can protect your creation by covering it with clear contact paper.

5. Display your *tzedakah* box somewhere in the classroom where you will see it and remember to fill it regularly with coins.

Grassroots *Tzedakah*

The possibilities for classroom-based *tzedakah* are as unlimited as your imagination. Here are a few general ideas, though you and your class can think up any number of others. Some of the activities below are described elsewhere in the book but can be applied to help others:

- Make get-well cards for the sick. (For instructions on making cards, see pages 20–21.)

- Make a meal or bake challah (see pages 6–8) and donate it to a homeless shelter.

- Make "care packages" for the elderly. Include fun things like a deck of cards, a joke book, slippers, lipstick, or lip balm.

- Have a function at your school as a fund raiser for a worthy cause. It could be a party, performance, carnival, yard sale, arts and crafts sale, or anything else that will attract people to come.

- Organize a basketball or softball game in your school or community, and invite the elderly to watch or underprivileged kids to play.

- Hold a two-on-two basketball tournament at your school or in your community and donate the entry fees to charity.

Mitzvot in the Community

Going beyond the classroom for *tzedakah* activities is a great way
to show kids how each of them is responsible for the welfare of
the community around them. Plus, it offers a terrific opportunity
for fun and educational outings.

Showtime at the Retirement Home!

Kids (and teachers) who are born performers will always have a
captive audience at retirement homes and assisted-living communities. The residents love visitors, especially young ones. Many
elderly people have children and grandchildren who live far away;
so having young people around is the next best thing to having
their own family near them.

Activities that students can prepare and perform together include:

- singing songs

- storytelling

- folk dancing

- putting on a play (based on a familiar story or one
  you've made up)

- making a puppet show

- giving an oral presentation on something of interest (for example, a really neat science experiment
  done for a school project)

Call the retirement home as far in advance as you can to
arrange a visit so the volunteer coordinator can put it in the
newsletter or put up signs to announce your activity. That way
you'll have a larger audience. Most places are quite enthusiastic
about these types of programs; they may even provide punch and
cookies or arrange a little party around the event.

If your students aren't the performing type, there are still ways
to "perform" a mitzvah at a retirement home. Some possibilities
include:

- making paintings and giving them to residents
- baking cookies for the residents (be sure to check first with the volunteer coordinator about any dietary guidelines you need to follow)
- donating books for residents to read to the kids

For the elderly, interaction with children is usually so enjoyable that even if you haven't had time to bake cookies or prepare anything, a visit is still appreciated. Sometimes just talking to residents and holding their hands is enough to brighten their day. Maybe a resident would like to watch a sports game on TV with students from your class or sit around the piano and sing. Some retirement homes have "adopt-a-grandparent" programs, where children are matched up with residents. That way, kids get to bring artwork and cookies to specific people on each visit.

Doing these sorts of activities at hospitals is also nice—whether a children's hospital or otherwise—though many hospitals are not as "performance-friendly" as retirement homes. Some don't allow visitors under age eighteen, while others have strict requirements that all volunteers go through volunteer training. Be sure to find out what all the rules are before you plan a class trip to a hospital.

Finally, when you've finished with your visit, talk with your students about the rewards of doing these kinds of activities. Discuss how it feels to do something nice for someone and how it helps the people you meet.

Some kids like to receive a certificate of achievement for doing the mitzvah. Teachers can buy the blank certificates at an office supply store (or download them from the Internet), fill them out, and even frame them. Or better yet, you can organize an arts and crafts activity around designing your own class's "mitzvah certificates," to be awarded whenever a student performs a good deed.

Special Trips to Special Homes and Shelters

Giving to the needy is always a good lesson for children, but rather than having the Salvation Army or Goodwill pick up items from your school, taking kids to drop off the donation in person makes for an experience they'll never forget.

Most homeless shelters, group homes for kids, and homes for battered women and children will accept several kinds of donated items: furniture, clothing, toys, and household items are usually greatly needed. Call beforehand to find out if they need the item you want to donate, and then arrange a time to deliver the donation with members of your class (the entire class might be too much for these places to handle).

While anonymous donations are a very special kind of *tzedakah*, it can also be rewarding for kids to visit the shelter where their donated toys are going so they can visualize and better understand this act of charity. Or your students can write a letter to leave with the donated toys, addressed to "Dear Friend" and including your school's address, so the child who receives the toy can write back. Besides donating items and money, your class can give of its time as well. Shelters usually need volunteers, especially in the kitchen. There are lots of ways to include kids, such as having them bake brownies in class and then serve the treats at lunch at the shelter, or encouraging them to design decorations for a holiday meal.

More Ways to Get Involved

Going out in the community to volunteer as a class—without an arranged group or organization sponsoring the event—is very important because it teaches children that they can make a difference on their own. In addition, there are agencies that have volunteer programs in which your students can take part and that offer good examples of how a larger community can come together to do a mitzvah.

Great sources for volunteering opportunities are local Jewish community centers or synagogues. Call to find out about programs, which may include helping recent immigrants adjust to life in the United States or trips to homeless shelters. Be sure to explain specifically what your class would like to do as volunteers, because some organizations may simply be looking for volunteers to work in an office or to make calls on the phone. While these are also worthy volunteering projects, they won't offer the same opportunities for young people.

One of the best sources for volunteer projects outside the Jewish community is your local branch of the United Way. It can direct you to groups like Habitat for Humanity, a national organization that helps to build suitable homes for low-income families. If your students have a specific area of interest (for example, the environment), the United Way can direct you to the organization that's right for you. Volunteering in that area of special interest will only add enthusiasm and enjoyment to the project.

Some other groups to know about:

- The Coalition on the Environment and Jewish Life (COEJL), a group providing a Jewish perspective on environmental concerns. Phone: 212-684-6950 x210; e-mail: info@coejl.org; website: www.coejl.org.

- Mazon: A Jewish Response to Hunger, a national organization that gives money to local groups that feed the hungry. Phone: 310-442-0020; e-mail: mazonmail@mazon.org; website: www.mazon.org.

15 Arts & Crafts—and Fun Things to Eat

Around-the-House Designs for Classroom Days

It doesn't have to be a holiday for your class to make Jewish crafts. There are plenty of opportunities for fun projects that are good to do all year round. Here's a whole bunch.

MEZUZAH MAGIC
Ages 5 and up

While no Jewish building is complete without a mezuzah on the front doorpost, you can also hang mezuzot (the plural of mezuzah) in the doorway of almost any room—including your classroom. Or kids can make a mezuzah to take home for their own bedrooms. These mezuzot make great gifts as well.

Here's a way to make a mezuzah from homemade clay. The special prayer scroll that goes inside each mezuzah can be purchased at Judaica stores. Besides this project, your class can use this clay recipe for all sorts of other things as well.

WHAT YOU NEED:

Materials
- cup salt
- 1½ cups warm water
- 4 cups all-purpose flour
- food coloring (optional)
- acrylic paints
- water-based sealer (nontoxic)

Equipment
- mixing bowl
- measuring cup
- toothpicks
- baking pan
- paintbrushes

HOW IT'S DONE:

1. Stir the salt into the warm water, and let it cool.

2. If you wish, add drops of food coloring to the water until it becomes the color you want. Otherwise, skip this step, and simply paint your mezuzah later.

3. Add flour to the water and knead it for 8–10 minutes until it has an even, claylike consistency.

4. Mold the "clay" into the shape of a mezuzah. Make sure you leave the back or inside hollowed out so you can fit the prayer scroll inside. And don't forget to leave two small holes at the top and bottom so you can nail the mezuzah to the doorpost. Other than that, it's entirely up to you how to shape your mezuzah: it can be long and thin, or wide and fat; it can have smooth edges or decorative sides. If you want, use toothpicks to scratch designs—such as Jewish stars or anything else you'd like—into the "clay."

5. Bake the mezuzah in the oven at 325°F for 30–60 minutes until the clay is completely dry and hard. Allow it to cool completely after you remove it.

6. Paint it any colors or designs you choose, and allow the paint to dry completely.

7. Cover the entire mezuzah (including the back) with water-based sealer, and allow it to dry.

8. Insert the scroll, and your mezuzah is ready to be nailed to a doorpost.

COSMIC JUDAICA: GLOW-IN-THE-DARK STARS OF DAVID

Ages 3–8

Who says you need to be outside to gaze up at the stars? Kids can take these Jewish stars home to shine above them on their bedroom ceiling. And they're all that much more fun when they make the stars themselves!

WHAT YOU NEED:

- white poster board
- scissors
- newspaper
- glow-in-the-dark paint (nontoxic)
- paintbrush
- double-sided adhesive tape

HOW IT'S DONE:

1. Draw Jewish stars on the poster board. They can be as large or small as you want.

2. Cut out the stars. (For younger kids, have them already cut out before the project begins)

3. Paint the stars with the glow-in-the-dark paint. Allow the paint to dry completely.

4. Cover the back of the stars with pieces of double-sided adhesive tape.

5. Stick the stars to the ceiling. (Children should let their parents take care of this step.)

6. Kids can turn off their bedroom lights and watch the stars glow.

PLAYFUL PLACE MATS
Ages 4–8

Since so many Jewish activities revolve around group meals and great food, personalized place mats are sure to get plenty of use. If your students are making place mats for themselves, let each of them design his or her own; if your class is making them for others, think of what sort of designs those people would like. You can also add the person's name in English or Hebrew.

If you'd like, design the place mats with specific holidays in mind; add symbols and pictures specific to that holiday (e.g., matzah for Passover, apples and honey for Rosh Hashanah).

WHAT YOU NEED:
Materials
- white posterboard (11" x 17")
- clear contact paper

Equipment
- crayons and markers (various colors)
- scissors

HOW IT'S DONE:

1. Using the crayons and markers, decorate the piece of posterboard.

2. Cut two pieces of contact paper slightly larger than the posterboard.

3. Unpeel one sheet of contact paper, and carefully lay it down on your work surface with the sticky side up.

4. Carefully lay your posterboard on the contact paper.

5. Repeat steps 3 and 4, covering the other side of the posterboard with contact paper.

6. If necessary, trim the edges of the contact paper.

7. Use your place mat for your next meal!

HOW TO GROW A FAMILY TREE
Ages 7–13

Here's a project that combines the fun of drawing, coloring, cutting, and pasting with the fascinating subject of family connections. Making a family tree lets children chart their family and maybe even learn something about their ancestors.

WHAT YOU NEED:

Materials

- scrap paper
- green construction paper
- poster board

Equipment

- thin-tip black marker
- pencil and eraser
- crayons, markers, or paint (brown and green, plus other colors)
- glue stick

HOW IT'S DONE:

1. Choose a set of grandparents or great-grandparents to be the root of the tree (you can do separate trees for each set of grandparents).

2. On a piece of scrap paper, list all of the sons or daughters that came from your "root couple," along with the husbands or wives of those children. Then, next to each of the sons or daughters, list all of the children that each of the sons or daughters had. Continue this until you reach the youngest generation in your family.

3. With the green construction paper, cut out one small leaf-shaped piece (approximately 2 inches) for each name you have on your list. On each leaf, write the name of one person on your list, proceeding until you have made a leaf for everyone.

4. On your poster board, sketch a large tree (do it first in pencil in case you mess up). Start with a wide trunk at the base, which

then splits into a branch for each child that the grandparents ("root couple") had. Each of those branches should then split into a smaller branch for each child they had, and so on until you have enough branches to account for the whole family.

5. Use crayons, markers, or paint to color the tree and the grass on the ground.

6. Paste the leaves with the names of the "root couple" on the trunk of the tree. Then on each branch that comes off the trunk, paste the names of their children, along with their children's husbands or wives. On each smaller branch, paste the names of the children's children, and so on until all the names have been pasted.

Tallit "Tie-Dye-enu"

When kids get to be bar/bat mitzvah age (thirteen years old), it's common for them to receive a *tallit*, the prayer shawl worn while in synagogue on Shabbat and holidays. There are many *tallitot* (the plural of *tallit*) available for purchase in Judaica stores and gift shops, but to have kids design their own *tallit* allows them to personalize it in a way that makes wearing it more fun and special.

The only requirement for a *tallit* is that it have four sets of *tzitzit* (tassels—that is, eight strings tied in a particular pattern on the four corners of the shawl). But other than that, there are no limits on how the shawl can look. One relatively easy way to design your own *tallit* is to tie-dye the shawl, using whatever colors and patterns you choose. For kids around bar/bat mitzvah age, making tie-dye *tallitot* makes for a terrific class activity.

Depending on how involved your students want to get in putting the whole thing together, this can be a great long-term project. It's a difficult challenge to go through the process of trimming the material, dyeing the fabric, and then tying on the *tzitzit,* but the thrill of having created a one-of-a-kind *tallit* makes the extra effort worthwhile.

SHAWL-OM
Ages 12–16

To make a *tallit,* start with a large piece of fabric to make into your shawl. Cotton is the least expensive and easiest to use, though silk also works well. The size of the fabric depends on the wearer. It should be about the length of the person's arm-span and anywhere from 12 inches to 36 inches in width, depending on the wearer's preference.

Fabric can be cut to size at a fabric store and comes in many patterns, though plain white is best for tie-dyeing. You'll need to hem the material to create a smooth edge. Or you can buy border trims and sew them onto the edges of the shawl.

It's also possible to find a large scarf in a department store or arts-and-crafts store that will already be hemmed and will be the right size. That will save you some time preparing the shawl for tie-dyeing.

The Hows-and-Whys of Ties-and-Dyes

Fabric dyes for tie-dye can be bought at arts-and-craft stores. If you buy a set of dyes, it will often come with complete instructions on how to tie-dye safely and without making a mess. If not, *make sure you get complete instructions* (more detailed than those here) *before you undertake dyeing.*

Basically, you'll need to mix the dyes with water, and depending on the type of dye you get, you may also need to add some other ingredients, such as soda ash and urea. (These may be included in a special tie-dye kit, or ask someone at the store where to get these ingredients.) In addition to the dyeing material, you'll need other supplies to keep the dyeing safe, tidy, and effective.

WHAT YOU NEED:

- rubber bands (to tie around the fabric to create designs)
- rubber or plastic gloves (to protect hands)
- newspaper or plastic lining (to cover your work area and protect surfaces from drips)
- buckets and bowls (to mix the dye in and/or for dipping the fabric into the dye)
- squeeze bottles or brushes (to apply the dye to the fabric if you don't want to dip the fabric)
- plastic bags (to put the fabric in afterward)
- plenty of paper towels or rags (to clean up)

Part of the fun and excitement of tie-dyeing is that you never know exactly how it will come out. Experimenting can lead to some amazing designs, though there are also techniques to help you create the design you want. Try some of these basic tying ideas.

HOW IT'S DONE:

1. Use rubber bands to block the dye from reaching certain parts of the fabric.

2. To create a symmetrical design, fold the fabric in half before doing anything else to it with rubber bands or folds.

3. To create stripes, pleat the fabric either vertically or horizontally.

4. To create a bull's-eye design, grab a bit of fabric from the center of the shawl, and tie it off with a rubber band. Tie more rubber bands lower down on the fabric "rope" you are creating. When you apply the dye, put colors between each rubber band.

5. Fold the shawl into triangles (the way flags are folded), and dip the corners into dye to create another interesting design.

6. Follow the dye manufacturer's instructions for drying the fabric and setting the dye. After you've applied the dye, put the shawl into a plastic bag and let it set for at least 3 hours (or overnight). Remove the fabric from the bag, and rinse it to get rid of excess dye. Then remove the rubber bands, and lay the fabric flat to dry.

All-Important Finishing Touches: *Tzitzit* and *Atarah*

Once your shawl is dyed and ready, you need to attach the parts that make the shawl into an official *tallit*. The *atarah* (collar, or "crown"), although not required, is found on nearly all *tallitot*. It is a thin strip (approximately eighteen inches long and two or three inches wide) that goes at the center of one of the long edges. This is the part that wraps around your neck when you drape the *tallit* around you.

The *atarah* can be decorated in many ways; often, the prayer you say when you put on the *tallit* is embroidered or written there (see Appendix of Prayers, page 202). Or you can simply put your name on the *atarah* and decorate it with glitter and paint (or perhaps you'd like to tie-dye it as well). Sew the *atarah* onto the shawl, or iron it on using two-sided fabric adhesive.

The final step in creating the *tallit* is to attach and tie the *tzitzit* strings to the four corners of the shawl. Create reinforced loopholes in the corners, ironing on patches there and then punching holes through the patches so that you can string the *tzitzit* through. *Tzitzit* can be purchased from a Judaica store, and they will come with directions on how to tie them. There is a very precise and involved way they must be tied (coiled seven, then eight, then eleven, then thirteen times, separated by double knots). It helps to have a second person assisting when tying.

Then you're ready to go. Congratulations!

Incredible Edibles

The only thing more fun than making a project with the whole class is making a project with the whole class ... and then eating it! Here are some fun and delicious activities.

ALL-PURPOSE CANDY CLAY
Ages 4–10

Make your classroom into a candy factory with this recipe. With only a few simple ingredients you can design sweets for any occasion:

shape them like a dreidel for Hanukkah; candlesticks for Shabbat; Jewish stars for Yom Ha'Atzmaut; or any other shape for other times of the year (flowers, hearts, etc.). They make great gifts, dinner party desserts, or snacks for around the house.

Note: For younger classes, the teacher should take care of steps 1–3.

WHAT YOU NEED:

Ingredients
- 10 ounces chocolate
- ⅓ cup corn syrup

Utensils (and supplies)
- saucepan
- nonstick pan or baking sheet
- waxed paper
- stirring spoon
- measuring cup

HOW IT'S DONE:

1. Over medium heat on the stove melt the chocolate in a pan, stirring until smooth (or follow package directions for microwave).

2. Add the corn syrup, and blend evenly.

3. Remove the pan from the heat, and pour the concoction into a shallow nonstick pan or onto waxed paper.

4. Once it has cooled enough to touch, spread it with your fingers into a sheet about ½ inch thick.

5. Cover with a piece of waxed paper, and leave it to stiffen for a few hours.

6. Once stiff, the candy clay can be molded into any shape you like.

"ME-SHUGGA" COOKIES
Ages 5–12

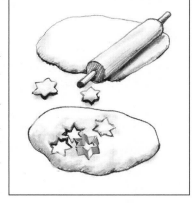

Sugar cookies are fun to make and eat any time of the year, but, if you can make them into Jewish cookies, they're even more special. (Some say they taste better, too!) Many Judaica stores or general gift shops sell cookie cutters in the shape of Jewish stars and other symbols.

If you're short on time, buy prepared cookie dough. It works well and tastes good. But if you want to make your cookies from scratch, here's a quick and easy recipe.

WHAT YOU NEED:

Ingredients

- ½ cup butter or margarine, softened
- 1 cup sugar
- 1 egg
- ¼ cup milk
- ½ tsp vanilla
- 2¼ cups flour
- ½ tsp salt
- 2 tsp baking powder
- colored sugar or cake gel

Utensils

- measuring cup
- measuring spoons
- 2 mixing bowls
- stirring spoon
- electric mixer
- bread board or smooth surface
- cookie cutters
- cookie sheet

HOW IT'S DONE:

1. In one bowl, stir the flour, baking powder, and salt.

2. In a second bowl, cream the butter and sugar together with an electric mixer; then add the egg, milk, and vanilla, and beat well.

3. Blend the contents of both bowls together thoroughly; then divide the dough in half and cover both halves with plastic wrap.

4. Chill the dough for 1 hour; then preheat the oven to 375°F.

5. On a nonstick (lightly floured) surface, roll the dough out flat so it is about ⅛ inch thick.

6. Using your cookie cutters (dip them into flour first to prevent sticking), cut the dough into the desired shapes.

7. Place the cut dough onto a cookie sheet, and decorate with colored sugar or cake gel.

8. Bake for about 10 minutes.

9. Allow them to cool down before gobbling them up! Makes about 40–45 cookies.

Adorable Adornments for Great Gifts

Whether it's for a *chag* (holiday), a *yom hooledet* (birthday), or any old reason, fun gifts and cards need fun wrapping paper and envelopes. And just as a gift is extra-special when it comes with a handmade card (for instructions on making cards, see pages 20–21), homemade wrapping paper and envelopes add an even more personal touch to the presents you give.

THAT'S A WRAP!
Ages 3–8

For the most part, making your own wrapping paper is quick and easy. The main trick is the decorations, for which we recommend you use paint stamps cut from sponges or potatoes. The shapes will depend on the occasion: cut a dreidel shape for Hanukkah, or queen's crown shape for Purim, or simply a Star of David for general purposes. What other shapes can your class think up?

WHAT YOU NEED:

Equipment
- scissors and knife (for use by grown-ups only)
- small dishes

Materials
- sheets of plain white paper (2' x 2' sheets are a good bet and can be found in art supply stores)
- sponges or potatoes
- tempera or poster paints (assorted colors as you like)
- paper towels
- metallic or other permanent markers (assorted colors)

HOW IT'S DONE:

1. Spread out one or more sheets of white paper.

2. Grown-ups can cut the sponge or one end of a potato into various shapes to use as stamps.

3. Soak some paper towel swatches in paint. Press the potato stamp or sponge stamp onto the paper towels and then onto the paper. Switch colors, shapes, and patterns to design your own custom-made wrapping paper.

4. Create additional decorations using the markers (see the Appendix of Stencils on pages 208–209 for ideas).

5. Let the paper dry, then use it to wrap up your gifts!

AND THE ENVELOPES, PLEASE ...
Ages 5–12

You'll never need to buy envelopes again. These do-it-yourself envelopes can be created in conjunction with do-it-yourself cards and wrapping paper—your students can impress their friends and relatives with their coordinated designs. Or they can send these envelopes with holiday or birthday cards.

WHAT YOU NEED:

Materials
- paper envelope (card or letter size)
- sheet of lightweight card-board
- brown paper grocery bags or construction paper

Equipment
- pencil, pen, or thin marker
- scissors
- glue stick

HOW IT'S DONE:

1. Taking care not to rip the paper, separate the folds of an envelope so that the paper becomes a single flat sheet.

2. Lay the unfolded envelope onto the cardboard, and trace around the edges of the envelope with a pen or marker to draw the shape on the cardboard.

3. Cut out the shape with scissors. (To save time in class, do this beforehand.)

4. Use the cardboard shape as a stencil to trace additional shapes onto the grocery bags or construction paper.

5. Cut out the shapes.

6. Fold the shapes in the same way that the original paper envelope had been folded (before you flattened it) to create new envelopes.

7. Glue the bottom and side flaps of the new envelopes down to secure the envelopes' pockets.

8. Decorate the envelopes with the same stamps and markers you used to design your cards or wrapping paper (see pages 120–121). Don't forget to leave some space on the front of the envelopes for the name and address.

16 Sports, Games & Outdoor Fun

Like a Maccabi
Ages 13–17

The Maccabiah is the "Jewish Olympics." Held every four years in Israel, it features the top Jewish amateur athletes in all age groups from all over the world. Events include everything from badminton to basketball, water polo to wrestling. Maccabiah athletes represent their country—but more importantly, the games represent Jewish solidarity throughout the world.

Even if no one in your class qualifies as a "Jewish Olympian," there are still many ways to get involved with Maccabi programs. Maccabi USA/Sports for Israel, which sends the U.S. delegation to the World Maccabiah Games, also sponsors U.S. teams to smaller competitions around the world. And the group supports even smaller local and regional Maccabi events of the Jewish Community Center (JCC) Association of North America.

The JCC Maccabi Games are open to Jewish teenagers ages thirteen to seventeen, regardless of athletic ability. Many local Jewish community centers around the country organize teams to take part in the regional Maccabi Games that are held each summer. Most JCCs have open tryouts. Contact your local JCC to get information on how your school can get involved. If you don't have a local JCC, contact the JCC Association.

If there are Maccabi Games planned in your area, your students' families can host visiting athletes. There's plenty of fun for everyone who takes part.

For more information:

- Maccabi USA/Sports for Israel, 1926 Arch Street
  4R, Philadelphia, PA 19103; phone: 215-561-6900;
  e-mail: maccabi@maccabiusa.com; website:
  www.maccabiusa.com.

- JCC Maccabi Games, JCC Association of North
  America, 15 E. 26th St., New York, NY 10010;
  phone: 212-532-4949; fax 212-481-4174; e-mail:
  info@jccmaccabi.org; website: www.jccmaccabi.org.

Jewish Scouting for Everyone

Like sports, scouting is a great way to get kids involved in outdoor
recreation. Just as the Maccabi Games work to reinforce Jewish
identity through sports, the National Jewish Committee on Scouting (NJCS) promotes Jewish identity through scouting. Joining
the Boy Scouts can be fun and enriching for Jewish boys as they
hike, camp, and learn important lessons about teamwork. Through
the NJCS, many schools, synagogues, and JCCs sponsor Boy Scout
troops. These groups are oriented toward Jewish scouts and may
add a Jewish slant to regular scouting activities.

Similarly, the National Jewish Girl Scout Committee, associated
with the Girl Scouts of the USA, encourages Jewish girls to get
involved in scouting. The organization sponsors programs and gives
out awards for Jewish Girl Scouts. It also arranges cultural exchanges
with groups like the Israel Boy and Girl Scouts Federation.

While scouting is generally done outside of school, teachers can
encourage Jewish scouting by providing information to their students. For more information:

- National Jewish Committee on Scouting, Relationships Division, Boy Scouts of America, 1325 W.
  Walnut Hill Lane, P.O. Box 152079, Irving, TX
  75015-2079; website: www.jewishscouting.org.

- National Jewish Girl Scout Committee, 33 Central Drive, Bronxville, NY 10708; phone: 914-738-3986; e-mail: NJGSC@aol.com; website: www.njgsc.org.

GO "GA-GA" FOR GA-GA

Ages 4–13

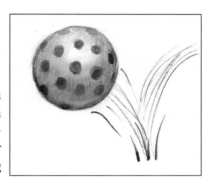

Ga-Ga is a popular kids' game in Israel and at Jewish camps. It's fun and easy but can also be an exciting, fast-paced game—perfect for the school gym or a small playing field.

WHAT YOU NEED:

- At least two players, though it's most fun with a large group.
- A ball (more than one can be used for large groups). Make sure the ball bounces well; it should be about the size of a basketball but softer (plastic bouncy ones are best).
- A playing area. Ga-Ga can be played indoors or outdoors, though playing within a limited (walled or fenced) area makes the game more fun.

HOW TO PLAY:

To start: A referee or leader bounces the ball in the center, and with each bounce all the players say "ga." After three bounces ("ga-ga-ga"), the ball is in play and any player may run up and hit it.

The object of the game is for players to hit other players with the ball below the knee. Any player hit by a ball below the knee is out.

Players cannot hit the ball with any other part of their body besides their hand and cannot pick up or throw the ball, or else they are out. If a player is hit by the ball above the knee, the player who hit the ball last is out.

If the ball goes out of play, there is a time-out. The referee or one of the players can go get the ball and start the game again by bouncing the ball in the center while others say "ga-ga-ga."

The last person left after everyone else has been eliminated is the winner.

Shesh-besh

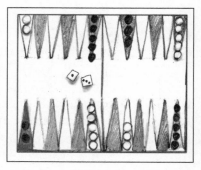

Shesh-besh is the Middle Eastern name for backgammon. This is the most common board game in Israel and all throughout the Middle East. The game is too complicated for very young kids, but it's lots of fun for older kids to play.

Shesh-besh involves two opponents who roll dice to move their playing pieces (called "stones") around a board while trying to block the other from doing the same. Basic math skills are required, and the more you play, the more you'll develop a sense of the strategy required to win this often fast-paced, highly competitive game. And if you get really good, you might even get up the nerve to challenge an Israeli to a game of *Shesh-besh*.

Backgammon boards, complete with dice, stones, and directions on how to play, are easy to find in stores where board games such as checkers and chess are sold.

"THIS CHALLAH'S-FOR-THE-BIRDS" FEEDER
Ages 3–8

Shabbat Shirah, the Sabbath on which the Song of Moses (Exodus 15) is recited, has traditionally been a time for Jews to reflect on and celebrate birds, who are said to sing the praises of God. *Shabbat Shirah* falls in the winter, and in some climates, birds (at least those that haven't flown south for the winter) are having trouble finding enough food to eat. What better way, then, to celebrate *Shabbat Shirah*—or to help out the birds any time of the year—than with an easy-to-make bird feeder?

Just like us, birds love challah (especially on *Shabbat*), so make the bird feeder out of leftover challah. Simply cover some pieces of challah completely with a thin coat of peanut butter. Then press the pieces into a dish of birdseed until they are completely covered with seeds. That's it!

Now all you have to do is find a place to put your challah bird feeder. Poke the pieces through a low branch on a tree (preferably one too thin for squirrels to get to), or simply place it in the tree securely. Then stand back and let the birds go to eat while you watch to see how many different kinds of birds come to visit your "this challah's-for-the-birds" feeder.

17 Jewish Music & Dance

The Classroom-Friendly Jewish Music Guide

Of the many great artists writing and recording music for Jewish families, we've gone through and picked out two dozen we think offer the best combination of fun (lyrics and music), accessibility, relevance, musical production quality, and educational value.

Though some of these artists have made other albums, the CDs we've noted are the best ones we know for classroom purposes. All of them include words and transliteration unless otherwise noted.

In addition to Judaica shops, music stores, and book stores, you can find many of these recordings online at www.amazon.com, www.jewishmusic.com, www.soundswrite.com, www.jewishstore .com, or other places. In some cases, you can also order the albums through the artists themselves, so we've included website information when available. In addition, www.totshabbat.com offers a huge list of artists doing Jewish kids' music, complete with sound samples and links.

Debbie Friedman

Friedman is probably the most popular composer, performer, and recording artist in the arena of American Jewish music, and her reputation is well earned. She consistently writes terrific songs, plus she has a beautiful voice and great Hebrew pronunciation.

Her most recent children's album, *The Alef Bet,* is a real treat. It's an outstanding collection of Friedman's most popular kids' songs for every day (as opposed to holiday-themed). These original Friedman compositions ("Alef Bet Song," "B'ruchim Habaim," "Im Ein Ani Li") are used widely in camps, schools, and synagogues across the country for good reason—they're both educational and so much fun! The album comes with an activity kit and songbook. We highly recommend it.

Shanah Tovah is an album that takes us through the year with terrific kids' songs for the Jewish holidays and some tunes for anytime. Our favorites include the calypso "Mah Nishtanah" and the exciting ragtime-style "613 Commandments."

Shirim Al Galgalim is a lively holiday album filled with songs that make you want to get up and dance. It's also quite prayer oriented with Friedman reciting many of the holiday blessings during the songs. The action-packed, New Orleans marching band–styled "Plant a Tree for Tu B'Shvat" and the country and western "L'Shanah Tovah" (which includes a shofar blowing) offer great melodies and simple lyrics that make it easy for young kids to sing along.

Miracles and Wonders, an album of Hanukkah and Purim tunes, features the Friedman classic "The Latke Song" (recorded by many others) and the funny "Haman's Song," about the ultimate bad guy. For Jewish classroom fun music, Debbie Friedman is the place to start.

www.debbiefriedman.com

Craig Taubman

My Newish Jewish Discovery features Craig Taubman, a fantastic musician, songwriter, vocalist, and performer, on what could be the coolest, hippest, and funniest Jewish kids' album you'll find anywhere! The album also manages to deal with important Jewish values such as being yourself, respecting parents, appreciating what you have, and playing fair. "My Mother Called Me a Name" and "A Candle in the Middle" are both funny and cute—and have surprise endings. Taubman's young daughter sings and Ed Asner reads a poem on the album. You're sure to sing along with the exciting, insanely energetic "Shigaon," and you may even learn a few Hebrew words in the process. Kids of all ages will love this album. Highly recommended.

My Jewish Discovery is also fun and full of great songs. "Holi-Daze," an exciting and hilarious rundown of all the Jewish holidays, sounds like a melody that would be in a Disney movie (not surprising, since Taubman has written music for Disney). "Hanukkah Rap," featuring hip-hop versions of Hanukkah classics (and lines like, "Go, Judah!… Judah's in the house!"), is great as well.

Taubman has also produced the delightful *Celebrate!* compilation boxed set, which includes three CDs *(Celebrate Shabbat, Celebrate Passover,* and *Celebrate Hanukkah)* with various Jewish recording artists, adding their best songs to the collection. And a new children's album called *Celebrate Kids!* is also a great compilation CD.

www.craignco.com

Cindy Paley

Paley is a talented and well-known performer of Jewish music with a beautiful voice and relaxed style that encourage the listener to sing along.

What a Happy Day is a lively collection of terrific everyday songs for young children. Many focus on teaching kids simple Hebrew words, and others are just for fun. Hebrew versions of "Old McDonald Had a Farm" and "If You're Happy and You Know It" are also included.

Zing Along with Cindy Paley collects Yiddish folk songs for children into an album that's well done, both vocally and instrumentally, with a terrific song selection. English narration and stories sprinkled throughout treat us to an entire performance of Yiddish culture. And kids are sure to get a kick out of the song "Oy Mayn Kepele," which includes the lyrics *"Oy mayn tushele* ("Oh my tush!") / Sing this little song / If you've been sitting down too long."

A Singing Seder offers a crash course in Passover melodies. It's a great way to brush up on old songs and learn some new ones, including some Israeli folk songs and the African-American spiritual "Go Down Moses." The album helps you through the whole seder.

Hanukkah: A Singing Celebration will put you in the mood for dreidels, menorahs, and latkes the moment you pop it into the CD player! This fun Hanukkah album includes the blessings as well as all the "Hanukkah classics." Paley introduces the Hebrew songs with a helpful one-line English explanation.

For Paley's full-on holiday treatment, check out her *Celebrate With Cindy* two-CD set, which compiles sixty songs from throughout the Jewish year.

www.cindypaley.com

Peter and Ellen Allard

We highly recommend the Allards' album *Sing Shalom: Songs for the Jewish Holidays*. Ellen Allard's lyrics are clever and catchy; her melodies are fun but also beautiful. Songs range in style from folksy sing-alongs ("Lotsa Lotsa Matzah") to rockin' ditties ("Judah Maccabee, the Hammer") to country and western square dance ballads ("The 15th of Shvat" and "There Are 10"). Then there's "Sukkat Shalom," a sweet, quiet song for Shabbat. Well-produced with great-sounding voices and instruments, the album takes us through the entire Jewish year. Plus, it's good for all ages. In addition to a number of secular CDs, Peter and Ellen have also recently released a CD called *Bring the Sabbath Home*.

www.peterandellen.com

Rich Glauber

The Soul Parade is not a well-known album, but it should be. Glauber, a talented musician and singer, approaches a wide range of values—including family, love, and diversity—in a way that's both smart and funny. While Glauber includes Bible motifs, Jewish foods, and Yiddish expressions, this is not a "religious" album. It takes a humanistic approach to Jewish culture with no mention of holidays or God. The song "Keep the Dream Alive" mentions Abraham and Sarah but also Martin Luther King and Rosa Parks. The song "Chicken Soup" is a hilarious Shel Silverstein–styled account of a boy's tenth birthday, when his grandmother made him eat every kind of Jewish food imaginable. This well-produced album may be too complex for preschoolers, but it is great for elementary age and up.

Sue Epstein

Nu!?!? From Sue: Fun Jewish Songs Little Kids Love to Sing is a well-produced CD with a real pop sound—very fun, happy, lively, and upbeat. In part, that's because Epstein has a fabulous voice; it's sweet and crisp even when she speaks. And the musicians are also great. Epstein includes a wide variety of songs, including some that are religious in theme (like her beautiful "Ki Eshmera Shabbat"). Except for a couple that are somewhat corny ("Kipah"), the songs (including "Hineh Rakevet" and "Mishpacha Song") are simply adorable.

I've Got That Shabbat Feeling is another feel-good album from Epstein. "I've been Polishing the Candlesticks" (to the tune of "I've Been Working on the Railroad") is classic Epstein: she's just so darn cute that you can't help but love her!

Shira Kline

Kline bills her debut CD, *ShirLaLa Shabbat!,* as "outrageously hip Jewish kiddie rock," and she's pretty close to the truth. The music manages to be bright and peppy without being cheesy, and the high production quality doesn't take away from the album's acoustic, down-to-earth quality. Fond of singing about "tushies," which will surely delight the little ones, Kline also covers the Shabbat sing-along basics—from game songs like "Chicken in the Pot" to *z'mirot* such as "Ki Eshmera Shabbat." And that's not to mention an inspiring rewrite of the classic "La Bamba" called "Shabbat Bamba." Kline, with her spiky hair and youthful sound, is a leading voice for a new generation of Jewish kids' music.

www.shirlala.com

Rabbi Joe Black

Black's *Aleph Bet Boogie* is a blast! It's filled with groovin' blues songs with Jewish themes and a sense of humor that your kids will really appreciate. The title song, "Aleph Bet Boogie," begins: "So you say you want to learn to be cool? That's easy. You go to Hebrew school." Other favorites include a rockin' "Build a *Sukkah*" and an energetic "Soufganiyot." Black is extremely likable and relaxed and ends the album by teaching us a few Israeli sing-alongs. He's having such a good time, it's impossible for listeners not to have fun as well.

Everybody's Got a Little Music is another good album from Black with standout tracks like the hilarious "Latke Hamentaschen Debate" and the country-style "Yodel Dreidel." The album combines fun songs with terrific instrumentation.

www.soundswrite.com/swjb.html

Rachel Buchman

On Buchman's Hanukkah CD *Shine Little Candles*, the liner notes say "Rachel Buchman is having a Hanukkah party and we're all invited!" That's exactly what this album feels like. Buchman is charming as she hosts this musical extravaganza. She does different character voices, tells stories, and sings a variety of Hanukkah songs in English, Hebrew, Yiddish, and Ladino. Buchman also chooses a nice group of guests for her party; on the album we hear from an older Yiddish-speaking couple, some Israeli parents, and a bunch of lively kids.

Guest kids and parents also show up on Buchman's *Jewish Holiday Songs for Children*, a twenty-three-song CD that is notable not only for its fine arrangements and performances but also for its unusual selection of mostly lesser-known holiday music, including songs for Lag B'Omer and Tu B'Shvat. Buchman also has CDs of secular children's music, including *Sing a Song of Seasons*.

The Shirettes

Never thought you'd see the terms "supergroup" and "Jewish kids' music" in the same sentence? Well, here it is: The Shirettes. Featuring seasoned performers Cindy Paley, Sue Epstein (two of our favorites), Judy Farber, Ditza Zakay, and Pearl B., the Shirettes combine their talents on *Friends B'Yachad* to create a wonderful twenty-six-song collection of all-around Jewish musical fun. The CD features a combination of songs that appear on the members' solo recordings—including favorites such as Epstein's "Shake Another Hand" and Paley's "Oy Mein Kepeleh"—and newly recorded group recordings. This is a great collection of some real pros in the world of Jewish children's music.

www.shirettes.com

Alan Eder and Friends

Reggae Passover is an enjoyably unique musical experience for all ages. Alan Eder, an expert in the area of African music, has produced a refreshing album that takes traditional themes of Passover and presents them in a quite untraditional way with West African and reggae instruments, rhythms, and melodies. Along with a large group of excellent musicians, Eder takes us on an exciting journey to a place where Passover's theme of freedom seems to fit right in. Eder also offers karaoke versions of six of the songs at the end of the CD so that your students can sing the lead vocals the next time around.

Reggae Hanukkah is another really good album of Eder's that we like almost as much. Besides the reggae, ska, and drumming found on the first album, there are also Middle Eastern, Brazilian, and Latin influences here.

www.reggaepassover.com

Tanja Solnik

Solnik's two CDs—*Generation to Generation: A Legacy of Lullabies* and *Lullabies and Love Songs*—are both beautiful collections of quiet Yiddish, Ladino, and Hebrew songs. Solnik's gorgeous voice makes it the perfect album to relax to—a Godsend for nursery school teachers during naptime. It includes Jewish lullaby classics like "Rozhinkes Mit Mandlen," "Durme, Durme," and "Numi, Numi."

www.tanjasolnik.com

Doda Mollie

Jewish educator Mollie Wine gets dolled up in flannels and bunny slippers for her very peppy and fun *Chanukah Pajamikah!* CD. Kazoos, slide whistles, harmonicas, banjos and assorted percussion keep the arrangements colorful, and her sense of joy is infectious. The song list features the usual lineup of Hanukkah material, but rarely have you heard it sound this fresh.

www.dodamollie.com

Paul Zim

Cantor Paul Zim, the self-proclaimed "Jewish Music Man," has been performing and recording Jewish music for years. He has several albums aimed at younger Jewish listeners that are quite entertaining. He's an enjoyable old-school Jewish performer—think Borscht Belt meets Barney. Spoken narratives often introduce his songs, and the choruses feature children's voices.

Zimmy Zim's Zoo includes eighteen songs about animals. There are classic Hebrew kids' songs like "Shubi Dubi" (about a teddy bear) and some folk songs in English like "Goin' to the Zoo."

The Kooky Cookie Kids is a sing-along album for preschoolers. The songs are cute: "Wiggle Your Fingers" asks kids to do motions as they listen to the song; "Put a Chicken in the Pot" (to the tune of "London Bridge Is Falling Down") is about preparing chicken soup for Shabbat.

If you like these albums Zim has many more, including *It's Jewish Holiday Time*, which takes us on a train ride through the Jewish year, and other children's recordings devoted to Shabbat, Hanukkah, Passover, and Israeli folk songs.

www.paulzim.com

Sally and the Daffodils

Tap Your Feet to a Jewish Beat is adorable. Sally Heckelman enlists a group of fourteen kids from her street—Daffodil Lane in Silver Spring, Maryland—to form her backup singers, the Daffodils. Her own children are in the group, and some of the kids' parents make guest-singing appearances as well. The album features twenty songs for Shabbat, holidays, and anytime, including a mix of songs by other contemporary artists, original arrangements of traditional songs, and completely original material. While the vocals are for the most part just average, the instruments—such as on the energetic "Hey Artzenu/Tzena" medley—are excellent and lots of fun. Sally and the Daffodils recently released a second collection called *Put a Smile on Your Face* that offers more of her joyful, intergenerational group singing.

Serenade

This group's album *Best of Serenade* is not specifically for kids, but we're listing it here because side two of the album is fantastic for Israeli folk dancing! It has all the most basic Israeli dancing songs, including songs to accompany some of the dances we teach you how to do (see pages 146–150). The album has been out for more than twenty years, but it's still the best one around that has all these songs ("Mayim," "Tsena Tsena," "Zemer Atik," "Tayish," etc.). There are no words or transliteration.

Sruli and Lisa

Face it, just about all klezmer music could qualify as kids' music— the joyful melodies and frenetic pace are sure to get children of all ages excited. But Sruli and Lisa take it one step further, by creating CDs—two so far, *Oy Vey!* and *Oy Vey! Chanukah!*—designed specifically to appeal to kids. Since klezmer is mostly instrumental, they do this by inserting goofy jokes and skits between songs— something that you'll either find enhances your enjoyment of the CD or else causes annoying disruptions to the beautiful music. At their best, though, Sruli and Lisa inject some extra humor and playfulness into the songs themselves, such as with a Yiddish version of "Old McDonald" called "Alter Motke," and their take on the Yiddish folksong "Az Der Rebbe," a follow-the-leader song that involves burping—it'll be a surefire crowd-pleaser in class.
    www.sruliandlisa.com

Fran Avni

Avni's *Latkes and Hamentashen* is presented like a storybook: Hanukkah on side one and Purim on side two, told with a combination of narration and original songs. The songs are all in English with cute, simple lyrics that are perfect for young kids. The album has an activity book to go along with it (sold separately).

The Seventh Day is a nice Shabbat album with a mix of familiar songs and great original ones. This album has a jazzy feel that's lots of fun, though it doesn't come with written lyrics. Avni also has CDs dedicated to Passover, Hanukkah, and Hebrew, as well as many secular kids' recordings.

www.franavni.com

Jill Moskowitz

Miracles: Hanukkah and Passover Songs for Kids features some of the very best and most singable songs for these two holidays. Moskowitz includes some traditional melodies, some originals, and some that other artists have made popular. The recording is simple but sweet with just Moskowitz's voice, a few instruments, and a group of young children singing along. "Lots of Latkes," sung in a round with the sounds of latkes frying, dreidels spinning, and Maccabees marching, is particularly fun.

Margie and Ilene

Just in Time for Hanukkah contains all the Hanukkah "classics" as well as the prayers. Margie Rosenthal and Ilene Safyan have beautiful voices and great Hebrew pronunciation with simple acoustic guitar and flute accompaniment. This is a wonderful album all students will enjoy. Margie and Ilene also have another CD called *All About Hanukkah* that comes with a book and includes explanatory narration between songs.

Around Our Shabbat Table includes beautiful songs that'll set the Shabbat mood in school. Many of the songs are somewhat formal, but there's also an exciting bluegrass "L'Cha Dodi" (set to the tune of "She'll be Comin' Round the Mountain") that's sure to get the whole class jumping!

www.sheeramusic.com

Peri Smilow

Songs of Peace starts with a terrific "Hineh Ma Tov" medley, ends with a very pretty "Sim Shalom," and contains lots of great songs in between. Smilow has a beautiful voice and is accompanied by lots of great musicians (drums, violin, clarinet, cello, horns, flute). She includes traditional Hebrew folk songs, some rearranged with original melodies and others set to familiar modern melodies (including a romping "Lo Yisa Goy" to the tune of "Down by the Riverside"). This is not specifically a children's album, but it's one kids are sure to enjoy.

www.perismilow.com

Myrna Cohen

Lullabies and Quiet Time starts out upbeat and lively, and though it gradually winds down we recommend it more for quiet-time than for actual naptime. She has a gorgeous, warm voice (though her Hebrew pronunciation is not great). It's terrific for preschool and early elementary school kids. Singing along with Cohen as she teaches us some Hebrew words *("Slicha, Toda, B'Vakasha")* and Jewish values *("Mitzvah Goreret Mitzvah")* is a group of young children. You can buy this on a double CD with another one of Cohen's recordings, *Special Days.*

www.soundswrite.com/swmc.html

Mark Bloom

Funky Punky Holidays, which features songs about the holidays and other Jewish themes, shows Bloom to be both a talented musician and a lyricist (though not particularly funky or punky). One particular favorite, "When You Speak a Little Yiddish," is a ballad about the Yiddish language; it's also nice when Bloom's children

make guest appearances on the album. His songs offer plenty of fun but also have a lot of words so they're better for kids over age ten.
www.markbloom.com

Robbo

A Part of a Chain: Fun Jewish Songs for Your Family is a well-produced album that tells stories from the Bible and deals with contemporary Jewish themes as well. "Tower of Babel" has funny lyrics, and Robbo (Robb Zelonky) provides theatrical performances throughout. Since he's a Hebrew school music teacher, he can get away with a song like "Hebrew School Blues," which is sung from a kid's perspective, whining about having to go to Hebrew school.
www.blanketkid.com

Kid-ish Yiddish Music

Yiddish can be a tough sell for young kids, since—unlike an earlier era—very few children grow up speaking or even hearing much Yiddish anymore. Still, there's great cultural value to the language, well worth keeping alive in Jewish life.

To that end, Yiddish music is a great way to make the language more approachable. A number of artists have recorded kids-oriented Yiddish music. The classic is still a 1957 album that Ruth Rubin made with folk legend Pete Seeger, *Jewish Children's Songs and Games*, which is still available (now on CD) through the Smithsonian's Folkways Records.

More recently, both the Lori Cahan-Simon Ensemble and Helene Engel have recorded kids-friendly Yiddish CDs. Both Engle's *Ay Lu Lu* and Cahan-Simon's *Songs My Bubbe Should Have Taught Me, Vol. One: Passover* (a second Hanukkah volume is on the way) feature wonderful, sophisticated arrangements and fascinating songs. *Ay Lu Lu*, however, seems more geared specifically for children with more nursery-rhyme type material and brighter orchestrations. What's more, Engel—a native of France now living in Montreal—sings many songs in English and French as well as Yiddish, which provides a convenient translation for kids to sing along with. (See also Cindy Paley's terrific *Zing Along with Cindy Paley*, reviewed above.)

Another recent favorite worth seeking out is *Di Grine Katshke (The Green Duck)*, a collection of Yiddish animal-songs for children, featuring members of the Klezmatics and other Jewish music notables. While, again, it's tough to capture kids' imagination with songs they don't understand, this CD is very well done, full of accessible songs that are beautifully played.

Kids' Favorites from Israel

Unlike the albums featured above, these popular kids-oriented recordings are made in Israel and feature mostly Hebrew songs. They're not as easy to find in regular music stores, but some Judaica stores have a nice selection of Israeli music.

Shlomo Gronich and the Sheba Choir

This Ethiopian children's choir sings beautiful Hebrew songs, often incorporating African-style melodies and rhythms. With a mix of popular Gronich originals and traditional tunes, this album is great for kids of all ages. Teachers will love it too!

Ofra Haza

With a gorgeously sweet voice and exotic style all her own, this popular Yemenite-Israeli music legend performs classic Israeli children's songs on *Songs for Children*. It's a really fun album that students and teachers will enjoy.

Ha Keves Ha Shisa Asar

This album, an Israeli version of *Free to Be You and Me*, is still popular more than twenty years after its release. Featuring songs written and sung by popular Israeli singers like Yoni Rechter, David Broza, Gidi Gov, Yehudit Ravitz, and Yonatan Geffen, it's a fun collection that's easy to sing along with and is geared especially toward young kids. Plus, sold separately, there's a picture book with the words to all the songs.

Festival Shirey Yeladim: Volumes 1, 2, 3

This is an outstanding collection of some of the most popular Israeli children's songs. These catchy tunes originated at the Children's Song Festivals in Israel, written and recorded in the 1960s and 1970s. They were recently re-released on this series of CDs, with new and old Israeli singers appearing.

Kool Klezmer and Alternative Jewish Music for Teens

While teens may feel like they've outgrown much of the children's and family-oriented music listed above, you'll be happy to know there are many great contemporary artists making Jewish-styled music that will surely appeal to older kids—and teachers as well. Modern groups are combining traditional Jewish sounds with jazz, rock, reggae, and even hip-hop to create some of the most exciting and eclectic music around today. Here's just some of the most listener-friendly "new klezmer" and other left-of-center Jewish music choices that are available through www.amazon.com (or other online record stores) or at your local CD store.

Klezmatics

Aside from the somewhat more traditional Klezmer Conservatory Band, this New York group is perhaps the best known of the contemporary klezmer bands, with members active in many areas (including KlezKamp, Living Traditions, and lots of sideline klezmer

bands). Of the group's many albums, *Jews with Horns* and *Rhythm and Jews* are the most fun. Though more oriented toward secular Yiddish culture than religion, many of the Klezmatics' songs offer subtle messages of tolerance and social action as well as a terrific combination of traditional (Hasidic melodies), folk (Yiddish labor songs), and contemporary popular music. The group's latest CD, *Rise Up!*, features a moving and inspiring Yiddish/gospel song ("Rise Up!") that calls out for people to take a stand against intolerance.
www.klezmatics.com

New Orleans Klezmer Allstars

Fresh Out the Past and *The Big Kibosh*, two of the widely available CDs by this talented young Louisiana instrumental group, are worth seeking out. There's not much that's overtly religious here (some of the band members are not even Jewish), but there are plenty of hip cultural references and great contemporary klezmer music that gets mixed with some wonderful New Orleans jazz. *Borvis* is the title of the group's most recent release.

Hasidic New Wave

A group headed by Klezmatics' trumpeter Frank London, Hasidic New Wave dedicates itself largely to creating brash and exciting (and sometimes noisy) modern jazz music with traditional Jewish melodies. Hasidic *niggunim*, as well as Ladino and *Mizrachi* (often translated as Middle Eastern and North African) elements, are combined with a healthy dose of irreverence (one song is called "Hebe Bop") on their albums, including *Jews and the Abstract Truth* and *Psycho-Semitic*. The group's latest CD, *From the Belly of Abraham*, is a collaboration with Senegalese drum ensemble Yakar Rhythms that's subtitled *Adventures of the Afro-Semitic Diaspora*.

Don Byron

This eclectic African-American clarinetist has, since his days with the Klezmer Conservatory Band, been one of klezmer's most accomplished musicians. *Don Byron Plays the Music of Mickey Katz*, his tribute to the popular klezmer musician from the 1950s, captures both Katz's "shticky" side ("Frailach Jamboree") as well as some seriously terrific playing. What's more, Byron's ability to cross cultures sends an important message about respect for the traditions of others and about music's power to overcome ethnic differences. (Unfortunately, he no longer plays klezmer as part of his live or recording repertoire.)

www.donbyron.com

King Django

King Django, a popular figure on the independent ska scene, investigates his Jewish heritage on the album *King Django's Roots and Culture*. With a combination of ska and reggae rhythms, klezmer touches, and Jewish themes, King Django offers a very cool take on some very old material (including a ska "Heveinu Shalom Aleichem").

www.kingdjango.com

Wally Brill

Brill's remarkable album *The Covenant* combines modern electronic "ethno-techno" music with samples from his collection of old 78-rpm records of famous early twentieth-century cantors. Cutting edge even by the standards of popular music, tracks like "Kiddush Le-Shabbat" (featuring Cantor Ben Zion Kapov-Kagen and an exotic "trance" rhythm) works as a tool for learning the Shabbat prayers and wouldn't sound out of place in a dance club either.

Zohar

Similar to Brill but even more sophisticated in its blending of cantorial music and dance beats with classical and Middle Eastern elements, the U.K. duo Zohar have released two terrific CDs, *Elokainu* and *One.Three.Seven*. Everything from the voice of famed cantor Moshe Koussevitzky and Israeli pop singer Zehava Ben to Arab and English vocalists combine with cutting-edge electronic music for cohesive, peaceful, and thoroughly contemporary music.

Knitting on the Roof

A wonderfully irreverent tribute to that most famous of Jewish musicals, this compilation comes courtesy of Knitting Factory Records, one of the best sources of weird and progressive Jewish music (also home to Hasidic New Wave). Underground favorites such as the Residents, Magnetic Fields, Eugene Chadbourne, and Negativland have their way with "Matchmaker," "If I Were a Rich Man," and others. The interpretations are not always completely successful, but they're always interesting.

Festival of Light (Vols. 1 and 2)

These compilations were marketed by mainstream record labels as Hanukkah albums, though only some of the songs actually have holiday themes. Still, there's a wide variety of Jewish-related music, with styles including alternative pop (They Might Be Giants), rock (Marc Cohn, Peter Himmelman with David Broza), New Age (Rebbe Soul), jazz (Don Byron), folk (John McCutcheon), and electronic (Wally Brill).

Divahn

OK, we're a little biased about this one—our sister/sister-in-law is the singer for this Texas-born, all-female quartet. Still, we believe the group plays some of the most thrilling and beautiful—and accessible, too—Sephardic and *Mizrachi* (Middle-Eastern) Jewish music you've ever heard. Their self-titled CD features many religious songs spiced up with Eastern melodies and contemporary arrangements. And, having been formed in Texas, they even add banjo and Southern gospel shadings to an Iraqi tune.

www.divahn.com

Oi Va Voi / Solomon & Socalled

This impressive new English sextet combines thoroughly modern electronic pop (call it trip-hop, chil-out, or whatever) with elements of Jewish and Eastern European music traditions. The group's debut album, *Laughter Through Tears,* is extremely well done, combining its disparate elements seamlessly. Oi Va Voi's violinist Sophie Solomon has also released a collaboration with Jewish Canadian hip-hop producer Socalled to create another interesting modern fusion CD called *HipHopKhasene.*

Israeli Folk Dancing: *Motza'ei-Shabbat* Fever!

As the state of Israel was forming in the 1940s, Israeli folk music and dances were made up on the spot as part of the whole new culture that was developing. You can feel the energy and excitement in these songs and dances and even in the ones that are still being created today. They combine the traditions of Jews that were coming to Israel from all over the world: Europeans, Yemenites, and Jews from other Arab countries.

These days, in many communities around the world, students can take part in Israeli folk dancing sessions at synagogues, universities, Jewish community centers, camps, or other organizations. Here are some simple Israeli folk dances and basic steps to get you going.

DANCE 101: BASIC STEPS

Tcherkessia (pronounced "chur-ka-ZEE-ah")

This step is based on an old Russian dance from the Tcherkessian (Circassian) mountains. The step has four beats, but your left foot stays in the same place during all four beats. (Imagine you have some gum stuck on your left foot as you hold it to the floor.) Start with your feet next to each other, facing forward. To count the four beats, you can say "chur-ka-zee-ah."

HOW IT'S DONE:

Beat 1: Step directly forward with your right foot.

Beat 2: Rock your weight back on your left foot. (Remember, don't pick up that foot!)

Beat 3: Step directly backwards with your right foot, behind your left foot.

Beat 4: Rock your weight again back to your left foot.

Repeat again and again.

Grapevine

This is the main step in many basic Israeli dances, including Mayim and Tzena. People also often do the Grapevine step in hora dances (or if you're not very coordinated, you can just run or jump around in a circle for the hora).

This step is like the Tcherkessia with four beats, but instead of keeping one foot planted, we're constantly moving toward the left. Start with your feet together, toes pointed forward, then move "front, side, back, side." Let your hips swivel, following your right foot naturally, "front, side, back, side."

HOW IT'S DONE:

Beat 1: With your right foot, step to the left, crossing in front of your left foot.

Beat 2: With your left foot, step to the left.

Beat 3: With your right foot, step to the left, crossing in back of your left foot.

Beat 4: With your left foot, step to the left, to end up as you started.

"Front, side, back, side. Front, side, back, side." Repeat this over and over.

STEPPING FORWARD: SOME EASY DANCES

Tzena

This dance goes along with the popular song "Tzena," which, if you don't know how it goes, is easy to find on Israeli music compilation albums (like the Serenade album, see page 137). The different parts of the dance go along with parts of the song, so it's much easier to learn this dance if you can sing along or listen to the music.

HOW IT'S DONE:

Section 1: Do eight sets of the Grapevine step, moving to the left (or clockwise in a circle).

Section 2: When the high part of the song begins, start with the right foot and skip to the right (counterclockwise around the circle) sixteen times.

Section 3: During the four strong beats of "Tze-na, Tze-na," bounce in place four times, then immediately go into three repetitions of the four-beat Tcherkessia step. Clap on the first beat of each Tcherkessia as you step forward.

Repeat section 3, then start from the beginning again.

Mayim

This is probably the best-known Israeli folk dance. When you have the music to follow along to (or can sing it), it's also easy to do.

HOW IT'S DONE:

Section 1: Do four Grapevine steps to the left.

Section 2: When the song goes, "Mayim, Mayim, Mayim, Mayim," start with your right foot and, with each of the four beats, take a step (so it's four steps) into the center of the circle, lifting your arms up as you go in toward the center. Clap your hands on the fifth beat as you step in place with your right foot. Then take four steps backwards with each beat, starting with your left foot, bending down slightly and lowering your arms as you move away from the center of the circle. (Imagine you are drawing the water, or *mayim,* out of the well as you come in and then spilling the water out as you move out.)

Section 3: When the song goes, "Hey! Hey! Hey! Hey!," turn to your left and, starting with the right foot, jog forward four steps (clockwise around the circle).

Section 4: On the next "Mayim, Mayim" section, bounce for eight beats on your left foot. Meanwhile with your right foot, step lightly forward, directly in front of your left foot on the odd beats (1, 3, 5, 7) and then lightly back to the right side on even beats (2, 4, 6, 8). After eight beats (step hard on the eighth beat), switch and do this with the opposite feet. Bounce on the right foot, stepping lightly with the left foot in front of the right, then back to the side, eight times. This time, clap on every odd beat.

Repeat the whole thing over again for the duration of the song.

Bottle Dance (Flasch Tanz, in Yiddish)

This is a stunt that would be done at weddings in Eastern Europe to fulfill the mitzvah of entertaining the bride and groom. Kids pick up this dance very quickly and love it. When you do the bottle dance at a wedding, you're not just showing off, you're entertaining! Practicing it in a classroom situation is sure to draw uproarious laughter from the students.

HOW IT'S DONE:

Step 1: Take a plastic liter bottle with a little liquid in it (maybe a fifth of the way full). Wear a hat that will allow the bottle to balance on your head.

Step 2: Place the bottle on your head and practice trying to stand still.

Step 3: Now practice walking carefully.

Soon you'll be able to progress to more difficult things, like moving side to side, jumping up and down, or squatting. Now you're doing the bottle dance. (And if all else fails, you can cheat by attaching the bottle to your hat with Velcro!)

Kozatzke

This is based on the Ukrainian dance of the Cossacks but has become a traditional Jewish dance over the years. Grab a friend or sibling, get in the middle of the circle at any bar mitzvah or wedding, do the Kozatzke, and you'll be the hit of the party! The dance takes two people.

HOW IT'S DONE:

Step 1: Grab a partner. Squat down and face each other.

Step 2: Extend arms in front of you, cross them, and hold hands— right hand to right hand and left hand to left hand.

Step 3: Each of you put your right leg out while keeping your left leg bent. Then quickly change so that your left leg is out and right leg is bent.

Step 4: Repeat this over and over as fast as you can, switching with each beat of the music if possible.

You can also do the Kozatzke by yourself with your arms crossed over your chest. But it's more fun to do holding on to someone else, and it's easier to learn that way.

18 Jewish Books & Stories for Class

Books Fun Guide

Jews are not known as "the People of the Book" just because of our deep connection to the Torah. The Jewish love of books extends beyond religious texts to include books of just about every kind—including great children's books. There have been thousands of books published that would be great additions to a classroom library, and obviously we couldn't include them all here. The books listed below are our suggestions of just some of the most fun Jewish kids' books widely available for purchase through book stores and online book sites (including www.amazon.com and www.jewishstore.com), or by contacting the publishers directly (see listing at the end of this section).

All-Around Fun and Adventure

... And Then There Were Dinosaurs, by Sari Steinberg (Pitspopany Press, 2003)

Using Claymation illustrations, this fable (based on Jewish legend) about the world God created *before* he created Adam and Eve will delight the hordes of kids who can't get enough about dinosaurs. Plus, it helps kids iron out what's often seen as a contradiction between the Genesis story and scientific evidence about dinosaurs. And it has a lesson to teach as well!

Brundibar, retold by Tony Kushner, illus. by Maurice Sendak (Hyperion, 2003)

Two acclaimed Jewish artists—playwright Kushner and author/
illustrator Sendak—team up to retell the story of the opera written and performed by prisoners at the Terezin concentration camp.
Jewish more in its subtext than in any overt way, it's nevertheless
a wonderfully soulful work.

Chicken Soup by Heart, by Esther Hershenhorn, illus. by Rosanne Litzinger (Simon & Schuster, 2002)

A charming tale, for kids three to eight, of the relationship between
a nice little *boychik* and his older neighbor, the "Chicken Soup
Queen." With attractive illustrations and a funny "old world" style
of storytelling, this story warms the heart and (thanks to a chicken
soup recipe at the end) warms the belly as well.

The Do-It-Yourself Jewish Adventure Series, by Kenneth Roseman (UAHC Press, 1993)

This terrific series of books, geared toward early teens, is designed
so that the reader is the main character and must make choices that
direct the course of the story. Depending on the choices, the story
can have many possible outcomes, making for an exciting read that
takes us on a firsthand tour through Jewish history. There are six
volumes so far, including *The Melting Pot: An Adventure in New York,
The Other Side of the Hudson: A Jewish Immigrant Adventure, Jeremi-
ah's Promise: An Adventure in Modern Israel, Until the Messiah Comes:
A Russian-Jewish Adventure,* and *The Cardinal's Snuffbox.*

Great Jews in the Performing Arts, by Darryl Lyman (Jonathan David Publishers, 1999)

More a reference text than something you'd read with your class
from cover to cover, this book has sections on one hundred different Jewish performing artists and small blurbs on two hundred
others. Included are Jerry Seinfeld, Adam Sandler, Roseanne Barr,
Tina Louise, Rosanna and Patricia Arquette, the Three Stooges, and
Harrison Ford (who knew?!).

Jews in Sports, by Joseph Hoffman, illus. by Janet Zwebner (Pitspopany Press, 1996)

A combination of factual histories on extraordinary Jewish athletes—from long ago as well as recently—and fun cartoon seek-and-find games, this book strikes a perfect balance to keep sports fans of all ages fascinated.

Jewish Heroes of the Wild West, adapted for young readers by Marion Maidens (Bloch/American Jewish Historical Society, 1997)

This is an adaptation for young readers of the book *Jews Among the Indians* by M. L. Marks. It tells the story of four Jews from the nineteenth century who played important roles in exploring and settling the West and who had close interactions with the Native Americans who lived there (one even became an Indian chief). Though the book is too complex for very young children, kids ages nine and up will find these stories very interesting.

The Moon, the Sun and a Hotdog Bun, by Mosh Kaposh, illus. by Eli Toron (Nava, 2002)

If Dr. Seuss was an orthodox Jew, his creations would've looked something like this book, which uses playful rhymes to tell about all the things that Hashem created.

The Story of the Jews: A 4,000 Year Adventure, by Stan Mack (Jewish Lights Publishing, 2001)

For older kids, particularly those who love comics, this book is a must-have. Famed cartoonist Stan Mack presents a brief but authoritative history of the Jewish people in comic book form from the time of Abraham up to the present day. With lively illustrations, an appropriate use of humor, and easy-to-follow explanations of some complex issues, the pages of Mack's history read quickly and stick with you afterward.

Wandering Stars: An Anthology of Jewish Fantasy & Science Fiction, edited by Jack Dann (Jewish Lights Publishing, 1998)

This unique book for teens and adults will thrill the science fiction fans in your house. Originally published in 1974, the collection of short stories features work by Isaac Asimov (who also writes the introduction), Bernard Malamud, Isaac Bashevis Singer, and more. With story titles like "On Venus, Have We Got a Rabbi," how can you go wrong? A second volume, *More Wandering Stars: An Anthology of Outstanding Stories of Jewish Fantasy & Science Fiction*, was published in 1999.

Favorite Folk Tales

The Adventures of Hershel of Ostropol, by Eric A. Kimmel, illus. by Trina Schart Hyman (Holiday House, 1995)

This colorful collection of ten Yiddish folk tales centered on Hershel, a legendary Jewish trickster, is a delight for children (ages four and up) and adults alike.

The Boy Who Stuck Out His Tongue: A Yiddish Folk Tale, by Edith Tarbescu, illus. by Judith Christine Mills (Barefoot Books, 2000)

This is a funny story of a naughty boy who sticks his tongue out one too many times—and gets it stuck to a wrought-iron fence. The whole town comes together to help free him.

Brainteasers from Jewish Folklore, by Rosalind Charney Kaye (Kar-Ben, 1997)

This book has a similar idea to *While Standing on One Foot,* but with shorter riddles and aimed for a slightly younger audience.

God Said Amen, by Sandy Eisenberg Sasso, illus. by Avi Katz (Jewish Lights Publishing, 2000)

A sweet, fanciful, and often funny story that everyone can identify with about the importance of meeting people half way. Based on an old Hasidic tale with delightful illustrations by our own Avi Katz, this book has a message for kids and grown-ups about not letting personal ego get in the way of what's best for everyone.

Golem, by David Wisniewski (Clarion Books, 1996)

This new version of the famous Jewish "Frankenstein" story is extremely well done—it even won the prestigious Caldecott Medal.

Older children will be thrilled by this monster tale, and adults will be surprised at how subtle and sophisticated it is. Younger children, however, will find it scary and perhaps even sad, so use discretion.

It Could Always Be Worse: A Yiddish Folk Tale, by Margot Zemach (Farrar Strauss & Giroux, 1990)

A favorite Jewish folk tale with a sly lesson of how everything—even misfortune—is relative. Well-illustrated and told for young readers.

Joseph Had a Little Overcoat, by Simms Taback (Viking, 1999)

A Caldecott Medal winner, this richly detailed, ingeniously designed book adapts the old Yiddish folk tale about how to make "something from nothing." It's essentially the same story as *Something from Nothing,* which we also recommend in this section, but the books vary in execution and are wonderful for different reasons. You probably don't need both, but you won't go wrong with either.

A Journey to Paradise and Other Jewish Tales, retold by Howard Schwartz, illus. by Giora Carmi (Pitspopany Press, 2000)

This collection of magical folklore draws from all over the Jewish world. Some of the tales can be a little scary for younger children, but they will ignite the imagination of school-age kids.

Seven Animal Stories for Children, by Howard I. Bogot and Mary K. Bogot, illus. by Harry Araten (Pitspopany Press, 1997)

Each of these short stories teaches a different value such as respect, modesty, or honesty. "Thinking thoughts" at the end of each story encourage further discussion between teacher and student. Recommended for children ages five and up.

Something from Nothing, by Phoebe Gilman (Scholastic, 1992)

A clever retelling of this touching Yiddish folk tale of how to make something from nothing, this will delight children of any age. A wonderful side story involving mice (told in pictures) provides even more fun.

While Standing on One Foot: Puzzle Stories and Wisdom Tales from the Jewish Tradition, by Nina Jaffe and Steve Zeitlin, illus. by John Segal (Henry Holt, 1996)

A great collection of eighteen stories that keep readers involved in the action by asking them to solve puzzles and come up with solutions to challenging and thought-provoking questions. Terrific for reading with kids ages eight and up.

Bible Stories and More

Adam & Eve's First Sunset: God's New Day, by Sandy Eisenberg Sasso, illus. by Joani Keller Rothenberg (Jewish Lights Publishing, 2003)

Sasso tells the story of what happened at the end of Adam and Eve's first day, when the sun goes down and the pair wonder if they'll ever see it again. It's a beautiful, and artfully illustrated, story for ages four and up, dealing with the fear of darkness and the wonder of renewal.

The Book of Miracles: A Young Person's Guide to Jewish Spiritual Awareness, written and illustrated by Lawrence Kushner (Jewish Lights Publishing, 1997)

A great book for kids nearing bar and bat mitzvah age to share with their parents, this slim volume conveys the relevance and beauty of Jewish values and belief through parables, *midrashim,* and examples drawn directly from biblical texts. Written in a straightforward but sophisticated style (for kids ages ten and up), the book manages to be simple and clear without talking down to smart kids.

But God Remembered: Stories of Women from Creation to the Promised Land, by Sandy Eisenberg Sasso, illus. by Bethanne Andersen (Jewish Lights Publishing, 1995)

With four stories about women mentioned only briefly in the Bible or known through *midrashim,* this book relies on the author's imagination to flesh out the important roles female heroines played behind the scenes in biblical times. Each tale points to a greater lesson about Jewish values, suggesting why these women should be remembered.

Daughters of Eve: Strong Women of the Bible, by Lillian Hammer Ross, illus. by Kyra Teis (Barefoot Books, 2000)

Talk about Girl Power! This book tells the stories of eleven women whose names may not be very prominent in the Bible but are very strong role models for girls and women of today. We hear stories about Miriam, Zipporah, Ruth, and more. For ages ten and up.

Does God Have a Big Toe? Stories About Stories in the Bible, by Marc Gellman, illus. by Oscar de Mejo (HarperCollins Children's Books, 1993)

Not actually Bible tales, but rather modern *midrashim* (amplifications of Bible stories), older kids (ages eight and up) will love these funny, smart stories that provide fresh meanings and new understandings of age-old tales. Gellman did a sequel called *God's Mailbox*.

The Illustrated Jewish Bible for Children, retold by Selina Hastings, illus. by Eric Thomas and Amy Burch (DK Publishing, 1997)

A great resource for overviews of Bible stories and other fascinating information about life during biblical times, this large volume is best suited for kids nine and up. Full of photos, illustrations, and maps that bring the stories to life.

In Our Image: God's First Creatures, by Nancy Sohn Swartz, illus. by Melanie Hall (Jewish Lights Publishing, 1998)

A beautifully told tale of how the animals and all that God had created took part in determining what humans would be like. Adapted from the biblical story of humankind's creation, it illustrates how all things are connected in nature.

The Jewish Children's Bible, adapted by Sheryl Prenzlau (Pitspopany Press, 1999)

This five-volume set (available separately or as a boxed set) offers readers ages eight to twelve a user-friendly overview of the five books of Moses, told concisely in contemporary language and accompanied by insightful commentary.

The Kids' Cartoon Bible, by Chaya M. Burstein (Jewish Publication Society, 2002)

The author of *The Jewish Kids' Catalog* offers a fairly concise comic-book version of the Bible, from Genesis all the way through Chronicles. This easy-to-digest retelling is perfect for kids eight and up.

King Solomon and the Queen of Sheba, by Blu Greenberg and Linda Tarry, illus. by Avi Katz (Pitspopany Press, 1997)

This is a story of interracial marriage in the Bible. King Solomon and the Queen of Sheba meet, fall in love, get married, and conceive a child but then have to go their separate ways. With beautiful illustrations, this book imagines how the Jewish religion might have come to Ethiopia.

Noah and the Great Flood, by Mordicai Gerstein (Simon & Schuster, 1999)

Gerstein's retelling of the Bible's Noah tale is augmented with details drawn from folklore and the author's own imagination. The additions make the tale even more magical and entertaining (featuring giants and made-up creatures), and they add new layers of meaning. Gerstein also has a great version of the Jonah story called *Jonah and the Two Great Fish,* and both books are suitable for kids ages four and up.

Sefer Ha-Aggadah: The Book of Legends for Young Readers, by Seymour Rossel, illus. by Judy Dick (UAHC Press, 1998)

This is an English translation and adaptation for young readers of the classic work compiled by Hayim Nahman Bialik, which covers Bible legends and tales of the sages. A rich and important work of Jewish/Hebrew literature, this is a wonderful addition to any classroom library. (An activity book supplement is also available.)

Tasty Bible Stories, by Tami Lehman-Wilzig, illus. by Katherine Janus Kahn (Kar-Ben, 2003)

Kids about eight and up will enjoy the way this lighthearted book combines freshly told Bible stories with easy-to-make recipes that relate to each story.

Why Noah Chose the Dove, by Isaac Bashevis Singer, illus. by Eric Carle (Farrar Strauss and Giroux, 1999)

The great Jewish literary figure and the much-adored children's book illustrator team up to tell a variation on the story of Noah's ark. Along the way, the story imparts an important message about humility.

Why the Snake Crawls on Its Belly, by Eric Kimmel, illus. by Allen Davis (Pitspopany Press, 2001)

A midrash on the Adam and Eve story to explain how snakes came to be the slithering, skin-shedding creatures they are. Great for the many younger kids who think snakes are a pretty cool subject for a book.

Israel Exploration

Agnon's Alef Bet, by S. Y. Agnon, illus. by Arieh Zeldich (Jewish Publication Society, 1998)

While it inevitably loses a little bit in the translation (letter "bet" stands for "house"), this classic children's work by one of Israel's most beloved literary figures is a wonderful introduction to the Hebrew alphabet.

The Great Israel Scavenger Hunt, by Scott E. Blumenthal (Behrman House, 2003)

For kids eight and up going on a trip to Israel (or just wanting to feel like they are), this book provides a fun guide to the country through the adventures of Daniel and his cousin Rivka. Plus, games and activities along the way make it truly an interactive tour book.

Ilan Ramon: Israel's Space Hero, by Barbara Sofer (Kar-Ben, 2004)

A biography, geared toward older schoolchildren, of Ilan Ramon, the first Israeli astronaut. From his childhood in Israel to his training in Houston to his tragic death in space, the book draws a complete picture of the life of this Jewish hero.

Jerusalem of Gold: Jewish Stories of the Enchanted City, retold by Howard Schwartz, illus. by Neil Waldman (Jewish Lights Publishing, 2003)

Schwartz has released many books collecting folk tales from throughout the Jewish world. Those collected here deal specifically with Jerusalem, and come from places including Iraq, Greece, and Poland. While the book might be too text-heavy to keep the attention of younger kids, those ages eight and up will find much to spark their imagination.

Snow in Jerusalem, by Deborah da Costa, illus. by Cornelius Van Wright and Ying-Hwa Hu (Albert Whitman, 2001)

This is a wonderful and touching story of two boys, both living in Jerusalem's Old City but still worlds apart. Avi lives in the Jewish Quarter; Hamudi in the Muslim Quarter. When the boys discover they're both caring for the same stray cat, will they be able to agree on how to share what they both love so much? The story is simple, but the implications are profound.

Holiday Treats and Treasures

Chocolate Chip Challah and Other Twists on the Jewish Holiday Table: An Interactive Family Cookbook, by Lisa Rauchwerger (UAHC Press, 1999)

From the chocolate chip challah of the title to Rock-a-My Sole Fish to Yentl (Lentl) Soup, this cookbook offers fun recipes for every holiday and Shabbat. In addition to the author's reminiscences about her grandmother and others who taught her to cook, space is left for you to write your own family recipes and thoughts. Plus, there are two accompanying activity books that are sold separately.

Drawing Your Way through the Jewish Holidays, by Eleanor Schick (UAHC Press, 1997)

A great source for the budding Jewish artist, this book takes you step-by-step though the process of making realistic drawings of many common holiday symbols, including candlesticks, Kiddush cups, seder plates, and more. It's appropriate for all ages but is best suited for kids over age seven.

The Family Treasury of Jewish Holidays, by Malka Drucker, illus. by Nancy Patz (Little, Brown, 1994)

This great book offers a taste of just about everything that's found in the other books in this holiday section. There are stories—new and traditional—recipes, songs, crafts, and information about all the major Jewish holidays and Shabbat. A terrific collection with lots for everyone to enjoy and something for all ages.

Fun with Jewish Holiday Rhymes, by Sylvia Rouss, illus. by Lisa Steinberg (UAHC Press, 1992)

The many holiday-related rhymes found in this attractively designed book will delight young kids and make everyone laugh.

Jewish Holiday Games for Little Hands, by Ruth Esrig Brinn, illus. by Sally Springer (Kar-Ben, 1995)

This activity book offers pictures and instructions on how to play holiday-related games and provides game pieces and boards when necessary. Activities like "Put Mordecai on the King's Horse" (a variation of "Pin the Tail on the Donkey") offer simple fun with a basis in the story or traditions of the holiday. Kar-Ben has an entire *For Little Hands* series, great for young children. Specific topics include Israel, High Holy Days, Hanukkah, and Passover, plus a special holiday crafts volume.

My Jewish Holiday Fun Book, by Ann D. Koffsky (UAHC Press, 2000)

This slim workbook features pictures to color, puzzles and mazes to complete, cut-out projects, and other activities relating to each holiday and Shabbat. If you use this book correctly, its pages will be ripped out, drawn on, and colored beyond all recognition by the time you're through.

Rivka's First Thanksgiving, by Elsa Okon Rael, illus. by Maryann Kovalski (Simon & Schuster, 2001)

As part of the young generation of new immigrants in America, Rivka must convince her family—and their rabbi—that Thanksgiving is a holiday for all Americans, Jews included. A heartwarming tale for kids four years old and up.

Shabbat Tales

Mrs. Moskowitz and the Sabbath Candlesticks, by Amy Schwartz (Jewish Publication Society, 1991)

Wonderful for all ages, this is the story of grandma's Shabbat candlesticks and how they inspire her to get a whole lot accomplished without even trying.

Too Much of a Good Thing, by Mira Wasserman, illus. by Christine Mannone Carolan (Kar-Ben, 2004)

Recommended for kids ages three to eight, this is a humorous tale of a king who loved the idea of Shabbat so much, he decided to make it last all week long. Of course, he soon finds out that a full week of Shabbat is just too much of a good thing, but one day is just perfect.

The Shabbat Box, by Lesley Simpson, illus. by Nicole in den Bosch (Kar-Ben, 2001)

Ira is thrilled that it's his turn to take the fun-filled Shabbat Box home from school. But he loses it in the snow, so he makes a new one to bring back to school on Monday. This is a gorgeously illustrated book with diverse faces and with a dad who's cooking Shabbat dinner. It also includes directions for making your own Shabbat Box.

Rosh Hashanah and Yom Kippur

Apples and Honey: A Rosh Hashanah Story, by Johnny Zucker, illus. by Jan Barger Cohen (Barron's, 2002)

An attractively illustrated overview of holiday practices and traditions, appropriate for young children. This book is part of a series that includes similar books on Hanukkah, Passover, and Purim.

Apples and Pomegranates: A Family Seder for Rosh Hashanah, by Rahel Musleah, illus. by Judy Jarrett (Kar-Ben, 2004)

Along the lines of the Rosh Hashanah seder offered in this book (see pages 18–20 and 205–209), this book goes even deeper in the seder by offering stories to accompany each of the special foods we eat as well as songs and recipes for the holiday.

Gershon's Monster, by Eric A. Kimmel, illus. by Jon J. Muth (Scholastic, 2000)

A chilling Rosh Hashanah tale, based in Jewish folklore, of Gershon the baker and how all the bad deeds he tried to sweep away grew to have serious repercussions. While younger children might be frightened by the book's monsters, older kids will be thrilled by this very exciting and very relevant moral tale.

The Hardest Word: A Yom Kippur Story, by Jacqueline Jules, illus. by Katherine Janus Kahn (Kar-Ben, 2001)

This story about the Ziz—a mythical giant bird who's so clumsy he knocks the stars out of the sky—will delight school-age children. Sent on a quest to find the hardest word to say, he finds it isn't "goodnight" or "spaghetti"—it's "sorry."

Rosh Hashanah: A Holiday Funtext, by Judy Bin-Nun and Franne Einhorn, illus. by Heidi Steinberger (UAHC Press, 1998)

This large and attractive book has a homemade feel to it, which is good because the activities inside will have you cutting out pages, drawing, and pasting all the way through it. The book is filled with simple activities for early school-age children.

Sammy Spider's First Rosh Hashanah, by Sylvia A. Rouss, illus. by Katherine Janus Kahn (Kar-Ben, 1996)

Sammy Spider lives in the home of the Shapiro family and enviously looks on as they prepare for Rosh Hashanah. Through Sammy, children learn about different customs of the holiday. Plus, this book teaches about sizes: big, middle-size, and small. This book is part of the Sammy Spider series, which includes books for Hanukkah, Passover, Purim, Tu B'Shvat, and even *Sammy Spider's First Trip to Israel.* All the books in this series are geared toward pre-school children.

Sophie and the Shofar: A New Year's Story, by Fran Manushkin, illus. by Rosalind Charney Kaye (UAHC Press, 2001)

Sophie's loud Russian cousin Sasha moves in next door. Ironically, after Sophie mistakenly accuses him of stealing her father's prized shofar, the two children end up forging a great friendship. Plus Papa lets them both try out his shofar!

When the Chickens Went on Strike, by Erica Silverman, illus. by Matthew Trueman (Dutton, 2003)

A wonderfully told and illustrated adaptation of Sholom Aleichem's short story "Kapores," which tells of how the village chickens managed to break their Jewish owners of a very inconvenient Rosh Hashanah tradition.

Sukkot

It's Sukkah Time, by Latifa Berry Kropf, photographs by Tod Cohen (Kar-Ben, 2004)

This bright book serves as a great introduction to Sukkot for very young kids (up to age four). In addition to photographs of *sukkah* building, decoration, and activities, the book includes Sukkot prayers and a fun mini-*sukkah* project. Other editions in this series include *It's Challah Time* and *It's Seder Time.*

Sukkot: A Family Seder, by Judith Z. Abrams, illus. by Katherine Janus Kahn (Kar-Ben, 1993)

With just the right amount of information (about fifteen text pages), this is a simple and terrific guidebook to a Sukkot seder—down to its own "four questions" about the holiday. The volume also includes *sukkah*-building instructions and sheet music for some songs.

Hanukkah

Dreidel, Dreidel, Dreidel, by Stephen Carpenter (HarperCollins, 1998)

Push a button, and this musical board book plays the popular Hanukkah dreidel song. Along with beautiful illustrations of kids playing dreidel and other Hanukkah scenes, the pages feature the lyrics to the song so that you can sing along as you read.

The Flying Latke, by Arthur Yorinks, art by William Steig (Simon & Schuster, 1999)

This whacky story tells about a humorously dysfunctional extended family gathering on Hanukkah. Among the more creative, off-the-wall holiday books on offer, it uses photo illustrations with real actors hamming it up on the page. Kids seven and up might just think it's hysterical.

A Hanukkah Treasury, edited by Eric A. Kimmel, illus. by Emily Lisker (Henry Holt, 1998)

A compendium of new and old stories, fun facts, songs, recipes, traditions, and games having to do with Hanukkah, all collected by one of the foremost Hanukkah authors. Great for kids of all ages. Kimmel has also written many terrific original Hanukkah stories, including *Zigazak, The Chanukah Guest, The Chanukah Tree, Hershel and the Hanukkah Goblins*, and *The Jar of Fools: Eight Hanukkah Stories from Chelm.*

Jason's Miracle, by Beryl Lieff Benderly (Albert Whitman, 2000)

This could be considered the boy's version of the book *There's No Such Thing as a Hanukkah Bush, Sandy Goldstein.* Secular Jewish pre-teen Jason wishes he could celebrate Christmas and thinks "So what!" about Hanukkah. Then in a dream he meets the Maccabees, who show him all they went through to keep Judaism alive.

Rainbow Candles: A Hanukkah Counting Book, by Myra Shostak, illus. by Sally Springer (Kar-Ben, 2001)

An adorable, colorful board book made especially for very young children, this gives kids practice in counting numbers up to nine and teaches the customs of Hanukkah. (Kar-Ben also has other Jewish board books, including *The Colors of My Jewish Year, My Jewish Home*, and *Shalom Shabbat: A Book for Havdalah.*)

The Runaway Latkes, by Leslie Kimmelman, illus. by Paul Yalowitz (Albert Whitman, 2000)

This adorable take-off on the Gingerbread Man fable features a rabbi, cantor, police, and others in hot pursuit of some runaway latkes whose absence threatens the upcoming Hanukkah party. A recipe and background information on latkes accompany this silly tale.

There's No Such Thing as a Chanukah Bush, Sandy Goldstein, by Susan Sussman, illus. by Charles Robinson (Albert Whitman, 1983)

Told from the perspective of a young secular Jewish girl who is always envious at Christmastime, this book is geared to preteens (ages nine to twelve). It delivers a nice message about appreciating the traditions of others without having to make them our own.

Tu B'Shvat

Listen to the Trees: Jews and the Earth, by Molly Cone, illus. by Roy Doty (UAHC Press, 1998)

A collection of environmental wisdom from Jewish tradition delivered in the form of poems, stories, and fun illustrations. Good for kids ages nine and up.

The Never-Ending Greenness, by Neil Waldman (Boyds Mills, 2003)

A beautifully illustrated book, for ages six and up, about a boy who escapes wartime Europe and comes to Israel, then plants trees that sprout into entire orchards to revitalize the land.

Noah's Wife: The Story of Naamah, by Sandy Eisenberg Sasso, illus. by Bethanne Andersen (Jewish Lights Publishing, 2002)

Written for kids ages four to eight, this modern-day midrash involves Noah's wife, whom God put in charge of collecting two seeds from every plant in the world so that they too would survive the flood. Naamah's story conveys a beautiful message about preserving and caring for all living things.

A Seder for Tu B'Shevat, **by Harlene Winnick Appelman and Jane Sherwin Shapiro, illus. by Chari R. McLean (Kar-Ben, 1984)**

This book, for kids ages four to eight, not only provides all the information your class needs to have a Tu B'Shvat seder but also includes interesting stories, songs, nature facts, and activities to further celebrate the holiday.

Solomon and the Trees, **by Matt Biers-Ariel, illus. by Esti Silverberg-Kiss (UAHC Press, 2001)**

This story, loosely based on biblical tales, tells of King Solomon's dedication to the trees of Israel. It imparts an environmental message while suggesting a possible origin for Tu B'Shvat. For kids ages four to eight.

Purim

Make Your Own Megillah, **by Judyth Groner and Madeline Wikler, illus. by Katherine Janus Kahn (Kar-Ben, 1998)**

In addition to providing information on the history and traditions of Purim, as well as instructions on making crafts, recipes, and games, this book includes seven pages that tell the *Megillah* story and are designed to be colored, cut out, and pasted together to make a long scroll. This book is perfect for kids ages four and up, but kids may require some help from teachers on certain crafts and recipes.

Queen Esther the Morning Star, **by Mordicai Gerstein (Simon & Schuster, 2000)**

Gerstein is the author and illustrator of many delightful Jewish children's books, and this one is no exception. It tells the story of the *Megillah* (the Book of Esther) in storybook form, accessible to children four and up.

The Whole Megillah (Almost), **by Shoshana Silberman, illus. by Katherine Janus Kahn (Kar-Ben, 1990)**

While not quite containing the whole text of the *Megillah*, this book features Hebrew excerpts from the Purim text as well as the English story for young kids. Plus it has songs, an entire Purim play script, and more ideas for adding fun to this already fun holiday.

Passover

A Different Night: The Family Participation Haggadah, by Noam Zion and David Dishon (Shalom Hartman Institute, 1997)

Though it is constructed more like a textbook than a fun book, this Haggadah is packed with information to enrich a seder. At nearly two hundred large-size pages, it's not the book you want to hand out to younger kids, but it is a great tool for teachers to prepare interesting and often humorous additions to an in-school seder.

The Energizing Haggadah for Children, illus. by Janet Zwebner (Pitspopany Press, 1998)

A standard Haggadah, in both English and Hebrew, but full of colorful cartoons, seek-and-find games, and puzzles for preteens (ages nine to twelve).

A Family Haggadah, by Shoshana Silberman, illus. by Katherine Janus Kahn (Kar-Ben, 1997)

This traditional Haggadah features the seder service on the right-hand page, while the left-hand page displays questions, commentaries, songs, activities, and games geared toward classes with younger children. A similar Haggadah by Kar-Ben, *A Family Haggadah II,* is also valuable but geared toward teens and adults.

Matzah Ball: A Passover Story, by Mindy Avra Portnoy, illus. by Katherine Janus Kahn (Kar-Ben, 1994)

When Aaron goes to a Baltimore Orioles game during Passover, he's upset he can't enjoy all the stadium junk food like the rest of the kids. As it turns out, though, bringing matzah to the ballpark is the best thing that could've happened to him. Appropriate for kids ages four and up.

Miriam's Cup: A Passover Story, **by Fran Manushkin, illus. by Bob Dacey (Scholastic, 1998)**

Written for kids ages four to eight, this beautifully illustrated book features a mother telling her daughter about Passover through the story of Moses' sister, the prophet Miriam. The idea of Miriam's Cup—a cup of water at the seder, similar to Elijah's cup of wine—is introduced as well (and lyrics to Debbie Friedman's song "Miriam's Song" are printed on the back).

My Very Own Haggadah: A Seder Service for Young Children, **by Judyth Groner and Madeline Wikler, illus. by Sally Springer (Kar-Ben, 1999)**

This coloring book takes young children (ages four to eight) through the Passover seder via easy-to-understand words and pictures.

Only Nine Chairs: A Tall Tale for Passover, **by Deborah Miller, illus. by Karen Ostrove (Kar-Ben, 1982)**

A fun and warmhearted story for all ages, written in rhymed verse, about a very familiar topic for families regardless of observance level: the overcrowded seder.

The Passover Seder: Touch, Turn, Open, and Learn!, **by Emily Sper (Scholastic, 2003)**

This overview of seder foods and traditions offers the kind of interactive lift-the-flaps, touch-the-textures stuff kids ages one to four love, packed with lots of information as well to get young readers familiar with Passover customs.

Shavuot

A Mountain of Blintzes, **by Barbara Diamond Goldin, illus. by Anik McGrory (Harcourt, 2001)**

Based on a folktale about Chelm, this charmingly illustrated story tells of a family's big Shavuot plan to cook up a pile of blintzes high enough to look like the mountain where Moses received the Ten Commandments. When other expenses take precedence, the entire family's cooperation is needed to round up the ingredients. For kids ages four to eight.

Contacting Jewish Publishers Directly

- American Jewish Historical Society: 781-891-8110; ajhs@ajhs.org; www.ajhs.org

- Jewish Lights Publishing: 800-962-4544; sales@jewishlights.com; www.jewishlights.com

- Jewish Publication Society: 800-234-3151; jewishbook@jewishpub.org; www.jewishpub.org

- Kar-Ben: 800-452-7236; custserve@karben.com; www. karben.com

- Pitspopany Press: 800-232-2931; pitspop@netvision.net.il; www.pitspopany.com

- Union for Reform Judaism (URJ) Press (formerly UAHC Press): 888-489-8242; press@urj.org; www.urjpress.com

Make Your Own Books

Reading books is a terrific activity that's fun, educational, and a great way of sharing experiences. But why not take it a step further and create your own book?

Depending on the age and interests of your students, self-made books can be a number of different things. They can tell the story of your students' family and ancestors, cover a topic of special interest, or rewrite a story from folklore. Or your students can make up a story of their own.

How much kids put into the book's design and construction is up to them: You can buy prebound notebooks and fill them with drawings, photos, and writing; or you can build books with construction paper, then bind them using string, yarn, or a store-bought binder; or take it to a print shop and have it bound into a spiral book. You can collect all the material beforehand (have students write the text or story on scrap paper first), or you can just make it up as you go.

Of course, the more planning that goes into the book, the better it will look in the end. But any book your students create will no doubt become an extremely valuable document they'll want to hold on to for years. What's more, it's a wonderful way to teach your students about books and expose them to ways they can express themselves through writing and art.

19 Jewish Films & Videos for Class

Videos and DVDs Fun Guide

It's not our intention to encourage your class to sit in front of the television when there are plenty of great hands-on learning activities to do. But everyone needs a little change of pace sometimes, and these videos offer some of the best Jewish children's entertainment around. It's possible to find some of these in Judaica stores or even regular video stores. Also, some Jewish community centers and libraries make them available to members, free of charge. But here are some other ways to order them: Kol-Ami (800-393-4264); www.jewishstore.com (888-597-8804); www.jewishvideo.com (877-539-4748); or Hataklit (800-428-2554 or www.shalom3000.com).

Shabbat and Holidays

Chanuka and *Passover at Bubbe's*

These two holiday programs are available together on DVD with a third, *Sing Along at Bubbe's,* which features songs from the two programs with lyrics. The series features Muppet-like characters learning about the holidays and singing songs—original ones as well as traditional Hanukkah and Passover favorites in Hebrew and English. The songs and stories explain various aspects of these two holidays and proclaim a general message to "be yourself." All three programs are also available separately on VHS.

Lights: The Miracle of Hanukkah

This terrific animated story, featuring the voices of Judd Hirsch and Leonard Nimoy, is simple enough for kids to enjoy but also sophisticated enough to fascinate adults. By symbolically equating magical Hanukkah lights with the light of Jewish spirit and learning, this video beautifully captures the essence of the Hanukkah story—if not the specifics—and also delivers an important message about everyone's right to be different. (VHS only)

Lovely Butterfly: Chanukah

This special Hanukkah episode of the Israeli children's program "Lovely Butterfly" features not only great animation but also puppets and people that play games and sing songs for the holiday. Though the overdubbing of English voices on top of the original Hebrew is somewhat distracting, overall the video is an enjoyable celebration of Hanukkah. (VHS only)

A Rugrats Passover

In this special episode of the extremely popular animated television series (and movies), the *Rugrats* kids learn about Passover from Grandpa Boris, who is trapped with them in the attic and missing the seder. While Boris tells the story of Moses and the Exodus from Egypt, three-year-old Angelica imagines herself as Pharaoh—and all the babies (including Tommy and Chuckie) as the Israelite slaves. When Tommy approaches her to "Let my babies go!" she finally meets her match. (The video also includes a bonus *Rugrats* episode, "Toys in the Attic.") (VHS only)

The Sabbath

This collection of four short films—featuring animation, clay characters, and live action—is an absolute delight. The joys, meanings, and importance of Shabbat are portrayed in funny ways that don't preach. The idea of Shabbat rest is presented in a very nice way. (VHS only)

Shari's Passover Surprise/Lamb Chop's Special Chanukah

Shari's Passover Surprise is a delightful Passover celebration with Shari Lewis, Lamb Chop, Charlie Horse, Hush Puppy, and some interesting special guests. Hush Puppy not only gets Dom DeLuise to cook the meal but also invites Robert Guillaume (a.k.a. "Benson") to the seder. As always, Lamb Chop and the other puppets are adorable. Plenty of musical numbers help tell the Passover story and explain the customs associated with this holiday. One highlight is a song performed by Guillaume, describing the story of the Ten Plagues. This show also emphasizes themes of diversity and the importance of inviting guests to our home on Passover. The Passover show is available together on one DVD with a similar Hanukkah episode starring Alan Thicke and Pat Morita along with Shari and the gang. Or both are also available separately on VHS.

Israel

Grandpa's Tree

This live-action short film, which follows an American musician on a quest to find the tree his grandfather planted years ago in Israel, is a great companion to Tu B'Shvat celebrations. Though somewhat corny and low on production values, it's a fun, music-filled story that covers the custom of the holiday as well as the institution of tree-planting in Israel. (VHS only)

Jinja's Israeli Safari

In Tel Aviv's Safari Park, Jinja, the adorable Israeli lion cub, takes us on a visit with the park's unusual animals, including ostriches, giraffes, and rhinoceroses. Though Jinja's voiced-over British accent can be hard to understand at times, and the video is more enjoyable if one can understand the funny Hebrew animal songs that are interspersed, children are sure to be thrilled with simply hearing the music and seeing the terrific live-action animals. (VHS only)

Songs and Stories

The Adventures of Agent Emes

Without doubt the first Hasidic secret-agent video series, *The Adventures of Agent Emes* depicts the heroic life of mild-mannered yeshiva boy Shimmy Epstein. Whenever the evil plans of Averos International get going, Epstein slips into his Agent Emes guise and saves the Jewish people from peril. This is some big-time Jewish kitsch, complete with corny humor, low-budget production values, and some stiff acting. But there are also elements of clever parody, and Jewish religion and values are always central to the plot. Though it's clearly most specifically geared toward orthodox Jews, more secular kids might find these adventures interesting as well. So far, two episodes have been made, and both are available on video, CD-ROM or by download (Episode One only) at www.agent-emes.com. They are:

- Episode One: The Fish Head
- Episode Two: Rabbi-Napped

Alef, Bet, Blastoff!

This is an outstanding series of eight video episodes that introduces children to traditional Jewish values in meaningful ways. It's not a religious production. Rather, it focuses on values and concepts such as being different, helping others, freedom, forgiveness, and welcoming strangers.

The main characters are two puppets, David and Rachel, children who are led on exciting adventures through time by the fearless Mitzvah Mouse. Together they meet some of the most important people in Jewish history. It's magical and musical, and there's always a nice moral at the end of the story. It's recommended for kids ages three to ten.

Each video runs approximately thirty minutes. You can buy videos individually, or the entire set together for less per episode (VHS only). The episodes are:

- 1: You've Come to the Right Place. Elliott Gould as Abraham.

- 2: Fixing the World. Ed Asner as Maimonides.

- 3: Lights of Freedom. Dom DeLuise as Pharaoh.

- 4: One Big Family. Lauri Hendler as Golda Meir.

- 5: A Hanukkah Mitzvah. Don Diamont as Judah Maccabee.

- 6: A Whale of a New Year. Avery Schreiber as Jonah.

- 7: A Light Unto the Nations. Cathy Ladman as Emma Lazarus.

- 8: The Whole Megillah. Erin Simms as Queen Esther.

Bible Stories for Children

Israeli author Meir Shalev and illustrator Yossi Abulafia bring the classic Bible stories of Adam and Eve, Noah, and others to life with humor and color. A very entertaining and well-made video. (VHS only)

Enough Already

An animated musical retelling of the wonderful folktale about a family who doesn't realize how good they have it. Through humor and klezmer music, the video overcomes its simplistic animation and gives an important lesson about being thankful for what we have. (VHS only)

Fliegel's Flight

This "bird's-eye view of Jewish history" is narrated by a cartoon bird named Fliegel, but in general this is not a cartoon. It's more like a documentary dealing with complex issues in Jewish history, including ancient and modern events, going all the way from Abraham up through Zionism and the Holocaust to the present day. Its themes are too complex for young children. But older students will find it both interesting and educational. (VHS only)

Shalom Sesame

This great series of videos (eleven in all) combines the popular American children's television show *Sesame Street* with Israel's version of it, *Rehov Sumsum*. Anyone familiar with *Sesame Street* will know what to expect: first-rate kids' programming that combines basic learning with humor that both kids and teachers will appreciate. There's a mix of animation, Muppets, and live action (featuring celebrities such as Sarah Jessica Parker, Joan Rivers, and Itzhak Perlman) with skits, songs, and educational shorts. The shows, approximately a half hour in length, can be bought individually or on longer videos that contain a bunch of episodes. The shows are:

- 1: The Land of Israel
- 2: Tel Aviv
- 3: Kibbutz
- 4: The People of Israel
- 5: Jerusalem
- 6: Hanukkah
- 7: Sing Around the Seasons
- 8: Journey to Secret Places
- 9: Aleph-Bet Telethon
- 10: Passover
- 11: Kids Sing Israel

Episodes 1–5, 6–8, and 9–11 are available grouped together or you can buy any of these eleven videos individually. (VHS only)

The Shirim K'tanim Song Festival

Terrific for kids of all ages, this hour-long video features thirty-three of the best Hebrew children's songs. The adorable combination of animation, claymation, and live action is a lot of fun. There are songs about holidays, Bible stories, and everyday situations.

With even the subtitles in Hebrew, the video is geared to kids who know some Hebrew. (VHS only)

Film Fun Guide

Here we list some mainstream Hollywood (or, in some cases, Israeli) films that were once shown on television or the big screen and are now available on video and/or DVD. While they are all good films with Jewish backdrops and elements, tastes will vary as to how appropriate they are for your class—and at what age your students should watch these films (while none have objectionable sex or violence, opinions will differ about their adult situations and moral messages). As with any film, teachers need to screen films first without students, then determine whether it is appropriate to watch in school.

An American Tail (1986, directed by Don Bluth)

An animated classic about Fievel, a young Russian mouse who searches for his family while adapting to his new home in America. The whole class will love this very sophisticated and exciting cartoon about the immigrant (Jewish) experience. Three sequels—*Fievel Goes West, The Treasure of Manhattan Island*, and *The Mystery of the Night Monster*—have also been made.

Exodus (1960, directed by Otto Preminger)

An exciting and heroic film adaptation of Leon Uris' historical novel set during the Israeli struggle for independence, starring Paul Newman. A rousing film filled with Zionist passion.

Fiddler on the Roof (1971, directed by Norman Jewison)

The classic film adaptation of the stage musical based on Sholem Aleichem's old country tales of Tevye. A "must see" for every Jewish kid.

Kazablan (1974, directed by Menahem Golan)

An entertaining Israeli musical (in both Hebrew and English versions) about a tough guy who tries to save his neighborhood from being torn down. A fun and interesting slice of Israeli life at the time with similarities to *West Side Story*, and a bunch of unforgettable songs.

Masada (1981, directed by Boris Sagal)

Originally a TV mini-series, this dramatic, inspiring, epic film depicts the struggle of a heroic Jewish desert outpost against the Romans.

The Outside Chance of Maximilian Glick (1988, directed by Allan A. Goldstein)

A meaningful family comedy about a young Jewish boy growing up in small-town Canada and the clash of cultures he encounters.

The Prince of Egypt (1998, directed by Brenda Chapman and Steve Hickner)

An animated retelling of the story of Moses and the Exodus from Egypt. Though it crams the story told in *The Ten Commandments*, a three and a half hour movie, into an hour and a half, its terrific animation and songs delight children.

Sallah Shabbati (1964, directed by Ephraim Kishon)

A lighthearted Israeli comedy starring Chaim Topol (who also plays Tevye in *Fiddler on the Roof*) as a recent Israeli immigrant who schemes ways to improve the situation for himself and his large family.

The Ten Commandments (1956, directed by Cecil B. DeMille)

A classic film that plays regularly on television, starring Charlton Heston as Moses, who grows up as Egyptian nobility only to reconnect with his Israelite roots and lead his people to freedom. This three and a half hour epic is a powerful, if somewhat sanitized and overacted, depiction of the defining moment of the people of Israel.

Yentl (1983, directed by Barbra Streisand)

An award-winning musical with Streisand directing and starring, this story is an adaptation of Isaac Bashevis Singer's short story about a young Jewish woman who, to study Torah, must disguise herself as a boy. Though it is sappy at times, families will find both the story and the music entertaining and meaningful.

Making Your Own Jewish Videos

Movies are not only something Jewish students can enjoy watching together, they're also something classes can actually make together. Producing home movies together gives children a sense that their own story is important and worth recording. And of course, it's tons of fun.

These videos will be precious documents that students will watch with their families for years to come. The possibilities are endless, but here are just some of the ways you can put your class in the movies:

- *Have students record their family's history.* Create a simple and low-budget documentary by having students film their parents, grandparents, and great-grandparents as they talk about their lives and what it was like to grow up Jewish in a particular time period. Instruct them on how to ask open-ended questions that will bring back memories in their relatives and to provoke complete and thought-provoking answers.

- *Film Jewish holiday observances.* Holidays are not only fun times to capture your class in action, they are times when you can record your class as it shares age-old customs. Because some Jews do not operate mechanical devices on religious holidays, filming activities in school (the days before a holiday) is a good time to catch students celebrating, or preparing to celebrate, holidays.

- *Film field trips, parties, and celebrations.* Any type of *simchah* is a great opportunity to shoot a Jewish kids' video.

- *Direct your own Jewish epics.* Your Jewish films can involve dressing up and acting out stories of your class's own creation. Cast your class in Bible stories, folk tales, or even stories that you make up yourself. Who knows, maybe the next Spielberg is in your class!

20 Internet & Software for Jewish Classrooms

Jewish Fun Webguide

Online Anytime!

Eileen's Favorite Camp Crafts and Other Fun Things! (www.chadiscrafts.com/fun/jewishcrafts.html)

Eileen knows her crafts, and this site combines all-purpose craft ideas and instructions with Jewish-related ones. The section titled "Jewish Crafts for Camps, Schools or Just for Fun at Home" provides some great projects, including clay mezuzahs and Jewish symbols made from beads.

Jewish Funland (www.bus.ualberta.ca/yreshef/funland/funland.html)

Run by Dr. Nurit Reshef, a Jewish educator in Alberta, Canada, Jewish Funland features a whole bunch of Java games, each with Jewish concepts, Israeli history and geography, or learning Hebrew. While all the games are great educational tools, they're also very oriented toward keeping kids entertained.

Jewish Funland games include an Israeli map puzzle that you have to slide into place (it's pretty tough!), two cute "Hebrew Hangman" games where you figure out Hebrew words commonly found in English (shofar, mezuzah) as well as Bible personalities, and a word match game where you connect pictures to their Hebrew and English names. There are also links to related sites devoted to Purim and Passover/Shavuot fun, a great Israel and Zionism game page, and a Bible challenge game page.

The J Site (www.j.co.il)

A simple but well-done site created by a Brooklynite-turned-Israeli, the J Site features lyrics to Hebrew songs, coloring pages, an Israel geography quiz game (which ain't easy!), a Hebrew sign maker, and a concentration-style match game. As much as the activities themselves, the site's use of Flash technology makes it a lively and interactive visit.

Jewish Jugglers Home Page (www.juggler.co.il/jews)

Juggling goes back to biblical times—who knew? This site, dedicated to Jewish jugglers, provides articles on the ancient Jewish history of jugglers (providing evidence from the Talmud) as well as information on great occasions for Jewish juggling and special tricks for Jewish jugglers.

Your Page (www.yourpage.org)

The "Kids Only" section of the Jewish National Fund's website features a bunch of simple Java-based games, puzzles, stories, crafts, and recipes that allow you to accumulate points as you go. Add to that a set of online greeting cards you can send to family and friends, and Your Page is one you'll want to visit again and again.

Zig Zag World (www.zigzagworld.com/games/home.htm)

This site is full of great games that use Java technology to teach Hebrew while having fun. The main feature is called "Hebrew for Me," which includes nearly a dozen variations on a basic "click and drag" feature that Java enables. In the "Around the House" game, for instance, players click on the Hebrew words for various pieces of furniture found at home, then drag a picture of the corresponding piece of furniture onto a larger picture of an empty house, which they then decorate.

Other "Hebrew for Me" games center around holiday themes, such as dragging the objects found on a seder plate onto an empty plate, or dragging holiday symbols onto a Hebrew calendar. In a playful, interactive environment, students learn Hebrew words by visually connecting them to pictures.

In addition, Zig Zag's site includes other educational games, including "AlefBetGo!"—where you slide Hebrew letters into order in a race against the clock—and "Why Don't Zebras Play Chess?," a word search puzzle.

Holidays in Cyberspace

Aish HaTorah Holidays (www.aish.com/holidays)

While the holiday page on Aish HaTorah's extensive website contains links to valuable information on all the Jewish holidays, the Hanukkah, Purim, and Passover links take you to activities that are specifically fun for kids. The sections for these three holidays include coloring pages to print out as well as holiday-related stories. The Purim page also includes jokes in Real Audio (though you and your students can be the judge of whether these actually qualify as jokes!). And the Passover page features a bunch of arts-and-crafts projects as well as some pretty fun ideas for the seder.

Billy Bear's Playground (www.billybear4kids.com/holidays/fun.htm)

Billy Bear's Playground is a mostly secular site with a wide range of fun material for kids. In the holiday section, the site includes pages dedicated to Passover and Hanukkah activities. The Passover activities include a Chametz game, mazes, and a word search. The Hanukkah page has a fun Java-run dreidel game, instructions for making a real dreidel, printable Hanukkah stationery, and special utilities that classes can use on their own websites (Hanukkah clip art, wallpaper, and icons).

HanuKat (www.hanukat.com)

This is a cute educational site where a feline by the name of HanuKat presides. As you'd expect, most of the material is focused on

Hanukkah—including stories, some great crafts (dreidel, menorah, origami), and activities. In addition, though, there is some similar material geared toward Passover.

Holidays on the Net (www.holidays.net)

You'll find lots of information on a wide variety of holidays at this site—Jewish holidays, secular holidays, and holidays of other religions. With each, you'll get the general background as well as articles on specific aspects of the holiday, plus activities, message boards, links to books, and other fun features. The page on the High Holy Days (Rosh Hashanah and Yom Kippur), for example, includes a Real Audio shofar that plays the sounds of the holidays at the click of a mouse (you must have a Real Audio player, which can be easily downloaded online).

Torah Tots (www.torahtots.com)

This extensive site features loads of educational and religion-oriented information on holidays, the Hebrew alphabet, and the week's Torah portion—all geared toward kids. The Holidays section offers general information, coloring pages that can be printed out and used for coloring (don't color on the computer screen!), "Fun & Games" that include a word search, a word decoder puzzle, and "plopples"—nonsense sentences that, when read aloud, sound like sentences that actually mean something (for example, on Rosh Hashanah: "Weed hipped he yap pull sinned tea hun knee"). Silly, yes, but fun for everyone involved.

Uncle Eli's Special-for-Kids Most Fun Ever Under-the-Table Passover Haggadah (www.acs.ucalgary.ca/~elsegal/Uncle_Eli/Eli.html)

This online version of the popular Passover book is not so much a usable Haggadah as a humorous commentary on the sections of the Haggadah. Uncle Eli's funny rhymes read like a Dr. Seuss book for smart-aleck Jewish kids (and the teachers who made them that way!).

Cool Sites for Kids and Teens (and Teachers Too!)

BabagaNewz (www.babaganewz.com)

This colorful site is the online extension of *BabagaNewz* magazine, a monthly publication geared toward young Jewish teens and distributed in classrooms. Plenty of activities are fun for middle-schoolers and their teachers. In particular, the Games section features a Mad Libs–type word game called Baba-Meisas, plus word searches and crossword puzzles, all of which can be done online. There's also a cool virtual tour of Israel using Quicktime.

Jewhoo! (www.jewhoo.com)

A play on the popular Yahoo! search engine, Jewhoo is an endlessly fascinating and often surprising clearinghouse of information about celebrities who are (David Arquette, Jack Black) and who aren't (Ben Affleck) members of the Tribe.

JewishSports.com (www.jewishsports.com)

This is a sophisticated site that offers information on a variety of Jewish sports topics, including in-depth articles on the latest exploits of prominent Jewish athletes. Plus, you can sign up to be on a JewishSports.com mailing list.

JVibe (www.jvibe.com)

This is a very hip Jewish site for teens that includes articles on popular culture, social action, politics, sports, and "real life," plus a chat area to let your opinions be known. Though clearly designed for teens—many of the articles are actually written by teens—adults will appreciate the site's sophistication and many of the articles as well.

SURFING THE HEBREW-NET: HEBREW FONTS ON YOUR COMPUTER

For those of us using English web browsers such as Netscape and Internet Explorer, surfing to a website that's written in Hebrew will more than likely turn up a bunch of gibberish that doesn't make sense in Hebrew or English. That's because our American browsers aren't equipped with Hebrew fonts that allow us to view Hebrew lettering on our computer screens.

The good news is that downloading Hebrew fonts onto your computer is extremely quick and easy. And once you download them, you'll open up a connection to an extensive network of Hebrew sites, many of them based in Israel, that provide a valuable link to the language and the land. If you know Hebrew, you'll be able to view up-to-the-minute news and entertainment from Israel; if you don't know Hebrew, it's a great way to help you learn.

HERE'S HOW TO DO IT:

1. Find a site that offers Hebrew fonts for download. Most of these sites will be Israeli sites where Hebrew is used. Look for a button that says "Can't see Hebrew?" or "If you don't see Hebrew, click here." Many Hebrew sites will have this feature (though often it will be written in Hebrew). Sites with English instructions for downloading Hebrew fonts include

   www.mct.co.il/hebrew.htm

   www.aiweinberg.com/hebrew.html

   www.huji.ac.il/unew/hebrew/hebrew.html

2. Determine which font to download, and click on the appropriate link. You'll probably have to choose between Windows versions and also between Netscape and Internet Explorer.

3. Save the file onto your hard drive, and note the folder in which you save it. The file should be executable (have an ".exe" suffix).

4. Go into your File Manager (if using Windows, go to Start, then Explore, to call up "Exploring" window) and find the file you downloaded.

5. Click on the .exe file you downloaded. The program will then lead you through a few prompts as it unzips the file and installs it onto your computer. Simply follow along.

6. If you are still online, you will probably need to close your browser, then open it up again for the new Hebrew font to be

usable. Otherwise, simply start up the browser and go surfing on the Hebrew-net.

Super Software

While there's hardly an unlimited selection, a fairly wide variety of software can be found for Jewish children—from more secular and entertainment-oriented to more religious and educational. The amount of fun your students have with each depends on their tastes and goals. The three main Jewish software manufacturers—JeMM, Davka, and T.E.S.—have websites (see end of chapter) that allow you to either order products directly or link to other sites where you can buy the software. In addition, www.jewishstore.com sells many of these products.

Holidays

Avner Travels in Time—Jerusalem 164 b.c.e. (T.E.S.)
Players join pint-sized hero Avner as he travels back in his time machine to help Yehuda the Maccabee liberate the Jews from the Greek army. This truly challenging and exciting game requires players to be both warriors, dodging enemy sentries, and scholars, learning about Hanukkah. The adventure game provides plenty of opportunity for fun and education for kids six to twelve years old. (Requires: Windows, 32 MB RAM, CD-ROM drive, sound card.)

Davka's Jewish Holiday Fun House (Davka)
Featuring four basic holiday-related activities with simple, spoken directions (no reading required), this CD is good for children as young as age three, if not younger. Arrange the pieces of a puzzle to reveal a picture, pick out which picture doesn't belong, match the picture with the holiday song, and click on a picture to learn more about the holiday—these easy-to-follow games offer holiday learning as one of a child's earliest computer experiences. (Requires: Windows, 8 MB RAM, CD-ROM drive, sound card.)

Hanukkah Activity Center (Davka)

A collection of eight Hanukkah activities, this CD includes a juke-box to play (and teach) holiday songs, a dreidel game, a trivia game, a coloring book, a "Nes-scape" web browser through Hanukkah history, and more. (Requires: Windows, 8 MB RAM, CD-ROM drive, sound card.)

The Interactive Haggadah (JeMM)

This program presents the Passover story through Claymation fig-ures from "The Animated Haggadah" video with sections for songs, traditions, and games. (What else? A computerized *afikomen* hunt!) The various sections can be explored in any order, making the dis-covery process individual to the explorer, and in your choice of three languages: Hebrew, English, or Russian. It's a great learning tool for kids before the seder, and a great interactive addition to this, the most interactive of all Jewish holidays. (Requires: Windows or Macintosh, 8 MB RAM, double-speed CD-ROM drive, sound card.)

Purim Rock! (JeMM)

Another gem from JeMM's holiday software series, this one uses Claymation figures to mount a full-scale rock opera that tells the Purim tale with songs in English or Hebrew. If you want a little more information, Scoop the spider fills in the plot details with humor and interactive bits. Plus there's a no-frills guide to the holiday's customs and history (more for adults than kids), as well as trivia and Purim songs to learn. (Requires: Windows or Macintosh, 16 MB RAM, double-speed CD-ROM drive, sound card, QuickTime 3.)

Shabbos with Shuki (Davka)

Davka's model Orthodox Jewish boy, Shuki, returns for his sec-ond CD-ROM. This time, kids can experience a full Shabbat with Shuki and family, from shopping and cleaning in preparation to Shabbat dinner prayers to synagogue services to Havdalah. As with the original "Shuki" release, users can choose between simply watching Shuki in action (best for very young kids) to directing his actions and playing related games. Great for Shabbat-observant (particularly Orthodox) children. (Requires: Windows or Macintosh, 64 MB RAM, CD-ROM drive, sound card)

Torah Targets (T.E.S.)

Knowing about the holidays is more important than ever when the survival of Earth depends on it. That's the situation in this game, which requires players to blast off into space and destroy the invading Space Blobs. To get ammunition, though, players have to correctly answer questions about the holidays. You can play with one or two "captains" and customize both game and question difficulty. But at any level this game is a real challenge and a fun learning tool. (Requires: Windows, 8 MB RAM, CD-ROM drive.)

Who Stole Hanukkah?! The Great Interactive Mystery Game (JeMM)

If your class thinks dreidel is fun, wait 'til you get your hands on this Hanukkah game, a CD-ROM whodunit that's both educational and extremely entertaining. The object: to figure out who stole Professor Croak's priceless jar of oil. Along the way, there are games, songs, and a cast of colorful characters. There are tons of useful information on the history and observance of Hanukkah that will appeal to older kids, while the animation and funny animals keep younger children amused. And be ready to spend some time with this one—solving the mystery isn't easy! (Requires: Windows or Macintosh, 16 MB RAM, double-speed CD-ROM drive, sound card.)

Fun and Jewish Learning

Avner & Brachot (T.E.S.)

Scrappy little Avner is the lead character in this great game, which is a long-form adventure, broken up into ten mini-games, with a heavy emphasis on learning the *brachot* (Jewish blessings). Kids six to ten will enjoy helping Avner find his way home by working his way through various challenges, and discovering the proper food blessings along the way. The CD also includes a reference guide to the *brachot* to use with or without the game. (Requires: Windows or Macintosh, 16 MB RAM, CD-ROM drive, sound card)

Davka Classic Game Pack I and II (Davka)

These CDs bring together Davka educational games previously (and sometimes, still) sold separately. The first collection includes Jewish IQ Basketball, which tests your abilities on the court—and in the field of Jewish learning. Mitzvah Mania challenges players to avoid obstacles and gather all the good deeds scattered on the screen while the clock is ticking. And Search for Your Israeli Cousin (also sold separately, see page 195) is a great way to teach older kids about Israel while having fun solving a mystery.

The second collection includes Hebrew Game Time (which includes Word Attack, Word Zapper, and Hebrew Hangman), Jerusalem Stones, a fast-paced Hebrew letter game, Search for Your Israeli Cousin II (see page 195), and Hanukkah Activity Center (see page 190). (Requires: Windows, 16 MB RAM, CD-ROM drive, sound card.)

Jewish Fact Attack (Davka)

Six basic computer games test kids' knowledge in areas of Jewish learning: "Holiday Hoops" uses basketball to match the Hebrew months and holidays, "Torah Toss" takes players to a carnival, where they must throw balls marked with names of Torah *parashot* into buckets marked with the corresponding book of the Torah, and so on. Many of the games will be too difficult for anyone not in a full-day Jewish school—some will even challenge the most learned of kids. (Requires: Windows, 16 MB RAM, CD-ROM drive.)

Mitzvah Man (T.E.S.)

Mitzvah Man—the Jewish version of Pac Man—feeds on knowledge. To keep him strong, players must answer questions dealing with Torah, ethics, and religious observances. There are levels for student and scholar. Because the game assumes a strictly Orthodox observance level in its questions, it's not designed for everyone. (Requires: Windows, floppy disk drive, sound card.)

Shuki (Davka)

Shuki is the model of what any Orthodox Jewish parents would want their little boy to be. This CD-ROM allows kids to see just how

Shuki does it—from waking up in the morning to say *"Modeh Ani"* to reciting the proper blessings to learning the aleph-bet at school. While younger kids can enjoy watching Shuki in action, slightly older kids can play along with games tied into Shuki's daily activities. Chances are, Orthodox kids will be most likely to connect with Shuki and enjoy this program. (Requires: Windows or Macintosh, 32 MB RAM, CD-ROM drive, sound card.)

Torah Tots Live! In Concert (T.E.S.)

This is the CD-ROM version of Torah Tots Live!, an Orthodox-oriented live stage show (as well as recording series) with life-size, cartoon-style characters—including Talmi D. Torah and Hardy Har Sinai—performing a full set of musical numbers such as "Lashon Hora" and "I've Got a Friend." The CD allows you to watch the show in its entirety or read the lyrics and sing along, karaoke-style. Plus there are coloring pages and a link accessing the Torah Tots website. (Requires: Windows, 32 MB RAM, sound card.)

Torah Tots: Parsha on Parade (T.E.S.)

The latest in an ever-expanding catalog of Torah Tots products, this series of software—still a work in progress—will eventually feature one CD-ROM for each of the five books of the Torah (as of now, *Bereishit, Sh'mot, Vayikra,* and *Bamidbar* are available, sold separately). Using the Torah Tots characters, the disc tells the story of each *parsha* (weekly Torah portion) in everyday language (though occasionally Hebrew terms are left unexplained). Each *parsha* also features games (decoding, word search, and a "Replace the Pickle" quiz), coloring pages (printable and on-the-screen), and a "Midrash Mavin" to give a little further information.

In addition to the *parsha* content, each CD-ROM includes a game show–style quiz on the entire book, an English translation of the biblical verses, and more puzzles in the "Teaching Materials" section. While the CDs feature the Torah Tots' usual Orthodox orientation—with Yiddish-style pronunciation and lifestyle assumptions that can be alienating to non-Orthodox Jews—the sheer amount of information provided will easily include something for everyone to learn and enjoy. (Requires: Windows or Macintosh, 16 MB RAM, sound card.)

Wisecrackers! (JeMM)

Designed for bar and bat mitzvah–age kids (the program even includes a Do-It-Yourself Bar/Bat Mitzvah Website Kit), Wisecrackers! is set up like a goofy game show, complete with a cheesy host and two players competing side by side. The object is to win all of the Jewish collectibles (including the world's only purple etrog and Jacob's wrestling shorts) by answering trivia questions. (Requires: Windows or Macintosh, 16 MB RAM, CD-ROM drive, sound card, QuickTime 4.)

Hebrew Games

Alef Bet Adventure (Davka)

This is far more of a straight educational tool than it is an actual game, but kids will likely find the lessons in Hebrew to be attractively presented and certainly challenging. Choose between learning about letters, vowels, and words—each section features lots to do. (Requires: Windows or Macintosh, 64 MB RAM, CD-ROM drive, sound card.)

The Alef Bet Word Book (T.E.S.)

This program, a combination of word search and coloring book, provides a great way for young kids to learn basic Hebrew words. Though it is a bit one-dimensional, its attractive visual display will help users create mental pictures to enhance vocabulary, while playing a challenging game. (Requires: Windows or Macintosh, CD-ROM drive.)

Hebrew Wordquest (T.E.S.)

Featuring two games—a Tetris-like game called Hebrew Wordmaster and a word search puzzle called Judaic Wordquest—this program offers a great way to build your Hebrew vocabulary and your comprehension of biblical terms while playing fun and challenging games. Because it requires a basic knowledge of Hebrew letters and reading, it is recommended for ages nine and up. (Requires: Windows, 4 MB RAM, floppy disk drive.)

Israel and the Bible

Noah and the Rainbow (Davka)

Based on the Judaica Press children's storybook of the same name, this CD version uses state-of-the-art animation, colorful graphics, and interesting sound effects to tell Noah's tale in rhyme. Full of humor and surprises, kids ages three and up will love experiencing this story as it unfolds on their computer screens. In addition to the story, the CD features a memory game, coloring book, and puzzle program. (Requires: Windows, 8 MB RAM, CD-ROM drive, sound card.)

Search for Your Israeli Cousin (Davka)

A clever way for older kids (ages ten and up) and adults to learn about Israel, this program takes you all over the Jewish state while you follow clues in search of your relatives. This race against the clock is not easy; you'll pick up tons of great information about Israeli cities along the way. With authentic Israeli music, funny characters, and beautiful photo-quality images, Israel is as close as your computer screen. (Requires: Windows, 8 MB RAM, CD-ROM drive, sound card.)

Search for Your Israeli Cousin II—Global Quest (Davka)

This sequel is even tougher (also for ages ten and up), taking you beyond Israel to search the entire Jewish world—from New York to Poland and nineteen other locations—for your lost relatives. Your students will learn about the history of Jewish life in cities around the world while following the clues and tracking down family. (Requires: Windows, 8 MB RAM, CD-ROM drive, sound card.)

Jewish Software Makers

- Davka: 800-621-8227; www.davka.com
- JeMM: info@ejemm.com; www.ejemm.com
- T.E.S.: 800-925-6853; www.jewishsoftware.com

Afterword

OK, then. If you've been following along, by now you've picked up some new ideas to help you and your students celebrate the holidays. You've worked with your class to help others, created artsy crafts and crafty arts, mastered great new games, and made a mess preparing tasty foods. You sang and danced along to cool music, flipped through the pages of classic books and stories, gave your "thumbs up" to terrific films and videos, and surfed your way through the Internet and software programs. What's no doubt clear at this point: there's no end to the possibilities for ways to inject some Jewish fun into (and outside) the classroom.

Adapt these activities to suit your classes' interests and tastes, and mix in your own custom-made ideas as well. It's not hard to figure out what's fun for the whole class. And when you're looking out for it, there's Jewish fun around every corner.

Appendix of Prayers

There are Hebrew prayers *(brakhot)* for every occasion—when you're sitting in a *sukkah,* washing your hands, even seeing a rainbow. Below is a list of prayers mentioned specifically in this book—some we included because they are not found in most prayer books; others we included because they're so common, we thought it would be nice to have a handy list of them right here. For others not listed below, check in any standard prayer book or ask a rabbi, cantor, or Jewish educator.

Shabbat Candlelighting

בָּרוּךְ אַתָּה יְיָ
אֱלֹהֵינוּ מֶלֶךְ הָעוֹלָם,
אֲשֶׁר קִדְּשָׁנוּ בְּמִצְוֹתָיו
וְצִוָּנוּ לְהַדְלִיק נֵר
שֶׁל שַׁבָּת.

Barukh attah Adonai
Eloheinu melekh ha-olam,
asher kidshanu bemitzvotav
vetzivanu lehadlik ner
shel Shabbat.

Praised are You, Adonai, our God, Ruler of the universe, whose *mitzvot* add holiness to our lives and who gave us the mitzvah to kindle the Shabbat lights.

Family Blessings

For the Sons

יְשִׂמְךָ אֱלֹהִים
כְּאֶפְרַיִם וְכִמְנַשֶּׁה.

Yesimkha Elohim
keEfrayim vekhiMenasheh.

(May) God make you like Ephraim and Menasseh.

For the Daughters

יְשִׂמֵךְ אֱלֹהִים
כְּשָׂרָה רִבְקָה רָחֵל וְלֵאָה.

Yesimekh Elohim
keSarah Rivkah Rakhel veLeah.

(May) God make you like Sarah, Rebecca, Rachel, and Leah.

For All Children

יְבָרֶכְךָ יְיָ
וְיִשְׁמְרֶךָ.
יָאֵר יְיָ פָּנָיו אֵלֶיךָ
וִיחֻנֶּךָּ.
יִשָּׂא יְיָ פָּנָיו אֵלֶיךָ
וְיָשֵׂם לְךָ שָׁלוֹם.

Yevarekhekha Adonai
veyishmerekha.
Ya'er Adonai panav elekha
vikhuneka.
Yisa Adonai panav elekha
veyasem lekha shalom.

(May) God bless you and watch over you. (May) God cause the
Divine face to shine upon you and be gracious to you. (May) God
lift up the Divine face toward you and give you peace.

Blessing over Wine

בָּרוּךְ אַתָּה יְיָ
אֱלֹהֵינוּ מֶלֶךְ הָעוֹלָם,
בּוֹרֵא פְּרִי הַגָּפֶן.

Barukh attah Adonai
Eloheinu melekh ha-olam,
boreh peri hagafen.

Praised are You, Adonai, our God, Ruler of the universe, Creator of the fruit of the vine.

Blessing for Handwashing

בָּרוּךְ אַתָּה יְיָ
אֱלֹהֵינוּ מֶלֶךְ הָעוֹלָם,
אֲשֶׁר קִדְּשָׁנוּ בְּמִצְוֹתָיו
וְצִוָּנוּ עַל נְטִילַת יָדָיִם.

Barukh attah Adonai
Eloheinu melekh ha-olam,
asher kidshanu, bemitzvotav
vetzivanu al netilat yadayim.

Praised are You, Adonai, our God, Ruler of the universe, whose *mitzvot* add holiness to our lives and who gave us the mitzvah of the washing of hands.

Blessing over Bread

בָּרוּךְ אַתָּה יְיָ
אֱלֹהֵינוּ מֶלֶךְ הָעוֹלָם,
הַמּוֹצִיא לֶחֶם מִן הָאָרֶץ.

Barukh attah Adonai
Eloheinu melekh ha-olam
hamotzi lekhem min ha-aretz.

Praised are You, Adonai, our God, Ruler of the universe, who brings forth bread from the earth.

Shehekheyanu

בָּרוּךְ אַתָּה יְיָ   *Barukh atah Adonai*

אֱלֹהֵינוּ מֶלֶךְ הָעוֹלָם,   *Eloheinu melekh ha-olam*

שֶׁהֶחֱיָנוּ וְקִיְּמָנוּ   *shehekheyanu vekiyemanu*

וְהִגִּיעָנוּ   *vehigiyanu*

לַזְּמַן הַזֶּה.   *laz'man hazeh.*

Praised are You, Adonai, our God, Ruler of the universe,
who has given us life and sustained us and enabled us to reach
this occasion.

Blessing over Fruit from a Tree

בָּרוּךְ אַתָּה יְיָ   *Barukh attah Adonai*

אֱלֹהֵינוּ מֶלֶךְ הָעוֹלָם,   *Eloheinu melekh ha-olam,*

בּוֹרֵא פְּרִי הָעֵץ.   *boreh peri ha-etz.*

Praised are You, Adonai, our God, Ruler of the universe, Creator
of the fruit of the tree.

Blessing over Food from the Ground

בָּרוּךְ אַתָּה יְיָ   *Barukh attah Adonai*

אֱלֹהֵינוּ מֶלֶךְ הָעוֹלָם,   *Eloheinu melekh ha-olam,*

בּוֹרֵא פְּרִי הָאֲדָמָה.   *boreh peri ha-adamah.*

Praised are You, Adonai, our God, Ruler of the universe, Creator
of the fruit of the ground.

Blessing over Food (Other Than Bread) from Wheat, Barley, Rye, Oats, or Spelt

בָּרוּךְ אַתָּה יְיָ
אֱלֹהֵינוּ מֶלֶךְ הָעוֹלָם,
בּוֹרֵא מִינֵי מְזוֹנוֹת.

*Barukh attah Adonai
Eloheinu melekh ha-olam,
boreh minei mezonot.*

Praised are You, Adonai, our God, Ruler of the universe, Creator of various kinds of nourishment.

Blessing over Other Food and Drink

בָּרוּךְ אַתָּה יְיָ
אֱלֹהֵינוּ מֶלֶךְ הָעוֹלָם,
שֶׁהַכֹּל נִהְיֶה בִּדְבָרוֹ.

*Barukh attah Adonai
Eloheinu melekh ha-olam,
shehakol nihyeh bidvaro.*

Praised are You, Adonai, our God, Ruler of the universe, at whose word all things come into being.

Blessing over the *Lulav*

בָּרוּךְ אַתָּה יְיָ
אֱלֹהֵינוּ מֶלֶךְ הָעוֹלָם,
אֲשֶׁר קִדְּשָׁנוּ בְּמִצְוֹתָיו
וְצִוָּנוּ עַל נְטִילַת לוּלָב.

*Barukh attah Adonai
Eloheinu melekh ha-olam,
asher kidshanu bemitzvotav
vetzivanu al netilat lulav.*

Praised are You, Adonai, our God, Ruler of the universe, whose mitzvot add holiness to our lives and who gave us the mitzvah to take up the *lulav*.

Blessing for Counting the *Omer*

בָּרוּךְ אַתָּה יְיָ
אֱלֹהֵינוּ מֶלֶךְ הָעוֹלָם,
אֲשֶׁר קִדְּשָׁנוּ בְּמִצְוֹתָיו
וְצִוָּנוּ עַל סְפִירַת הָעֹמֶר.

Barukh attah Adonai
Eloheinu melekh ha-olam,
asher kidshanu bemitzvotav
vetzivanu al sfirat ha-omer.

Praised are You, Adonai, our God, Ruler of the universe, whose
mitzvot add holiness to our lives and who gave us the mitzvah of
counting the *omer*.

Blessing for Putting on the *Tallit*

בָּרוּךְ אַתָּה יְיָ
אֱלֹהֵינוּ מֶלֶךְ הָעוֹלָם,
אֲשֶׁר קִדְּשָׁנוּ בְּמִצְוֹתָיו
וְצִוָּנוּ לְהִתְעַטֵּף בַּצִּיצִת.

Barukh attah Adonai
Eloheinu melekh ha-olam,
asher kidshanu bemitzvotav
vetzivanu lehit'atef batzitzit.

Praised are You, Adonai, our God, Ruler of the universe, whose
mitzvot add holiness to our lives and who gave us the mitzvah of
wrapping ourselves in *tzitzit*.

THE SEPHARDIC/PERSIAN ROSH HASHANAH SEDER

Blessing for Sweet Year/Apples and Honey

יְהִי רָצוֹן מִלְּפָנֶיךָ,
יְיָ אֱלֹהֵינוּ וֵאלֹהֵי אֲבוֹתֵינוּ,
שֶׁתִּתְחַדֵּשׁ (שֶׁתְּחַדֵּשׁ) עָלֵינוּ
שָׁנָה טוֹבָה וּמְתוּקָה.
מֵרֵאשִׁית הַשָּׁנָה
וְעַד אַחֲרִית הַשָּׁנָה.

Yehi ratzon milfanekha
Adonai Eloheinu Velohei avoteinu,
shetit'khadesh (shetekhadesh) aleinu
shanah tovah umetukah,
mereshit hashanah
ve-ad akharit hashanah.

May it be Your will, Adonai, our God and God of our ancestors, to renew this year for us with sweetness and happiness, from the beginning of the year to the end of the year.

Prayer with the Leek

יְהִי רָצוֹן מִלְּפָנֶיךָ,
יְיָ אֱלֹהֵינוּ וֵאלֹהֵי אֲבוֹתֵינוּ,
שֶׁיִּכָּרְתוּ אוֹיְבֶיךָ וְשׂוֹנְאֶיךָ
וְכָל מְבַקְשֵׁי רָעָתֵינוּ.
תָּרוֹם יָדְךָ עַל צָרֶיךָ
וְכָל אוֹיְבֶיךָ יִכָּרֵתוּ.

Yehi ratzon milfanekha,
Adonai, Eloheinu Velohei avoteinu,
sheyikartu oivekha veson'ekha
vekhol mevakshei ra'atenu.
Tarom yadkha al tzarekha
vekhol oivekha yikaretu.

°May it be Your will, Adonai, our God and God of our ancestors, that all evil in the world be cut off. Rise up against evil and put an end to it.

°*interpretation*

Prayer with the Beet

יְהִי רָצוֹן מִלְפָנֶיךָ,

יְיָ אֱלֹהֵינוּ וֵאלֹהֵי אֲבוֹתֵינוּ,

שֶׁיִּסְתַּלְקוּ אוֹיְבֶיךָ וְשׂוֹנְאֶיךָ

וְכָל מְבַקְשֵׁי רָעָתֵנוּ:

סוּרוּ מִמֶּנִּי כָּל פֹּעֲלֵי אָוֶן

כִּי שָׁמַע יְיָ קוֹל בִּכְיִי:

סוּרוּ סוּרוּ צְאוּ

מִשָּׁם טָמֵא אַל תִּגָּעוּ

צְאוּ מִתּוֹכָהּ

הִבָּרוּ נֹשְׂאֵי כְלֵי יְיָ.

Yehi ratzon milfanekha,

Adonai Eloheinu Velohei avoteinu,

sheyistalku oivekha veson'ekha

vekhol mevakshei ra'atenu.

Suru mimmeni kol po'alei aven

ki shama Adonai kol bikhyi.

Suru suru tze'u

misham tameh al tiga'u

tze'u mitokhah

hibaru nos'ei khlei Adonai.

°May it be Your will, Adonai, our God and God of our ancestors, that all evil in the world be wiped out. Remove all evil, because You, God, have heard the sound of my crying. Distance yourselves from evil and that which is impure. Cleanse yourselves, those who are followers of God.

°interpretation

Prayer with the Dates

יְהִי רָצוֹן מִלְפָנֶיךָ,

יְיָ אֱלֹהֵינוּ וֵאלֹהֵי אֲבוֹתֵינוּ,

שֶׁיִּתַּמּוּ אוֹיְבֶיךָ וְשׂוֹנְאֶיךָ

וְכָל מְבַקְשֵׁי רָעָתֵנוּ:

יִתַּמּוּ חַטָּאִים מִן הָאָרֶץ

וּרְשָׁעִים עוֹד אֵינָם

בָּרְכִי נַפְשִׁי אֶת יְיָ הַלְלוּיָהּ:

וּבְחַסְדְּךָ תַּצְמִית אוֹיְבַי

וְהַאֲבַדְתָּ כָּל צוֹרְרֵי נַפְשִׁי

כִּי אֲנִי עַבְדֶּךָ.

Yehi ratzon milfanekha,

Adonai Eloheinu Velohei avoteinu,

sheyitamu oivekha veson'ekhah

vekhol mevakshei ra'atenu.

Yitammu khatta'im min ha-aretz

ursha'im od einam

barkhi nafshi et Adonai halleluyah.

Uvkhasdekha tatzmit oivai

veha'avadeta kol tzorerei nafshi

ki ani avdekha.

°May it be Your will, Adonai, our God and God of our ancestors,
that all evil cease to exist. All evil should be wiped out from the
earth. Bless the Lord, oh my soul, halleluyah. And with Your
righteousness erase all evil, because I am Your servant.

°*interpretation*

Prayer with the Squash

יְהִי רָצוֹן מִלְפָנֶיךָ,
יְיָ אֱלֹהֵינוּ וֵאלֹהֵי אֲבוֹתֵינוּ,
שֶׁתִּקְרַע רוֹעַ גְּזַר דִּינֵנוּ
וְיִקָּרְאוּ לְפָנֶיךָ זְכִיּוֹתֵינוּ.

Yehi ratzon milfanekha,
Adonai Eloheinu Velohei avoteinu,
shetikra ro'a gezar dinenu
veyikar'u lefanekha zakhiyoteinu.

May it be Your will, Adonai, our God and God of our ancestors, to
tear up the evil decree against us, and let our good deeds present
themselves to You.

Prayer with the Beans

יְהִי רָצוֹן מִלְפָנֶיךָ,
יְיָ אֱלֹהֵינוּ וֵאלֹהֵי אֲבוֹתֵינוּ,
שֶׁיִרְבּוּ זְכִיּוֹתֵינוּ
(וּתְלַבְּבֵנוּ).

Yehi ratzon milfanekha,
Adonai Eloheinu Velohei avoteinu,
sheyirbu zakhiyoteinu
(Persian tradition: *utlabevenu*).

May it be Your will, Adonai, our God and God of our ancestors,
that our merits (*Persian tradition:* and our inspirations)
will multiply.

Prayer with the Pomegranate

יְהִי רָצוֹן מִלְּפָנֶיךָ,
יְיָ אֱלֹהֵינוּ וֵאלֹהֵי אֲבוֹתֵינוּ,
(שֶׁיִּרְבּוּ
זְכִיּוֹתֵינוּ)
(שֶׁנִּהְיֶה
מְלֵאִים מִצְוֹת)
כָּרִמּוֹן.

Yehi ratzon milfanekha,
Adonai Eloheinu Velohei avoteinu,
(Sephardic tradition: *sheyirbu*
zakhiyoteinu)
(Persian tradition: *shenihyeh*
mele'im mitzvot)
karimon.

May it be Your will, Adonai, our God and God of our ancestors, that (*Sephardic tradition:* our merits will multiply) (*Persian tradition*: we should be full of good deeds) like the seeds of the pomegranate.

Prayer with the Fish

יְהִי רָצוֹן מִלְּפָנֶיךָ,
יְיָ אֱלֹהֵינוּ וֵאלֹהֵי אֲבוֹתֵינוּ,
שֶׁנִּפְרֶה וְנִרְבֶּה כַּדָּגִים
וְתִשְׁגַּח עָלָן בְּעֵינָא פְּקִיחָא.

Yehi ratzon milfanekha,
Adonai Eloheinu Velohei avoteinu,
shenifreh venirbeh kadagim
vetishgakh alan be-aina pekikha.

May it be Your will, Adonai, our God and God of our ancestors, that we should be fruitful and multiply like fish, and You should watch over us with open eyes.

Prayer with the Lung

יְהִי רָצוֹן מִלְּפָנֶיךָ,
יְיָ אֱלֹהֵינוּ וֵאלֹהֵי אֲבוֹתֵינוּ,
שֶׁיִּהְיוּ עֲווֹנוֹתֵינוּ קַלִּים
כָּרֵיאָה.

Yehi ratzon milfanekha,
Adonai Eloheinu Velohei avoteinu,
sheyihyu avonotenu kalim
kere'ah.

May it be Your will, Adonai, our God and God of our ancestors,
that our wrongdoings will be light like the lung.

Prayer with Something from the Head of an Animal

יְהִי רָצוֹן מִלְּפָנֶיךָ,
יְיָ אֱלֹהֵינוּ וֵאלֹהֵי אֲבוֹתֵינוּ,
שֶׁנִּהְיֶה לְרֹאשׁ וְלֹא לְזָנָב
וְתִזְכּוֹר לָנוּ אֵילוֹ שֶׁל יִצְחָק
(אָבִינוּ עָלָיו
הַשָּׁלוֹם בֶּן אַבְרָהָם אָבִינוּ
עָלָיו הַשָּׁלוֹם).

Yehi ratzon milfanekha,
Adonai Eloheinu Velohei avoteinu,
shenihyeh lerosh velo lezanav.
Vetizkor lanu eilo shel Yitzkhak
(Persian tradition: *avinu alav*
hashalom ben Avraham avinu
alav hashalom).

May it be Your will, Adonai, our God and God of our ancestors,
that we should be like the head not like the tail. And for our benefit, remember the story of Isaac (*Persian tradition:* our forefather,
may peace be with him, son of Abraham our forefather, may
peace be with him).

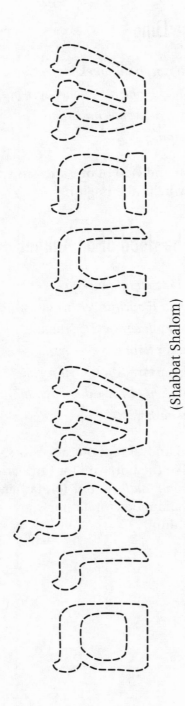

(Shabbat Shalom)

(Matzah)

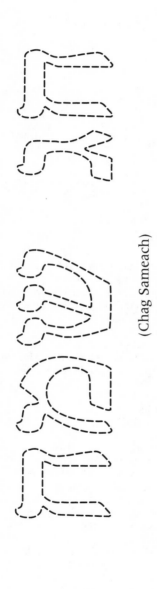

(Chag Sameach)

(Shanah Tovah)

209

Index

By Activity

books & stories
  bible stories and more, 156–59
  folk tales, 154–56
  fun and adventure, 151–54
  Hanukkah, 164–66
  holiday treats and treasures, 160–61
  Israel exploration, 159–60
  midnight read and feed, 84
  Passover, 168–69
  Purim, 167–68
  Rosh Hashanah and Yom Kippur, 162–64
  Shabbat tales, 162
  Shavuot, 169–70
  Sukkot, 164
  Tu B'Shvat, 166–67
computers & the internet
  Hebrew fonts on your computer, 187–89
  software, 189–95
  webguide, Jewish fun, 183–87
dancing
  basic steps, 146–47
  easy dances, 148–50
  Israeli folk, 146–50
  Tu B'Av, 90

don't Lag B'hind, 80
decorating
  flowers, a house blooming with, 86
  tips for the *sukkah* "interior decorator," 26–27
dress up
  backwards day, 61
  costume department, the, 54–55
  dress up and lie down, 69
  open up! it's Elijah, 71–72
films, 179–81
games
  dreidel-playing basics, 38–39
  Shesh-besh, 126
gardening
  by phone or keyboard, 49
  classroom, 48–49
  herbs, easy-to-grow for your *besamim* box, 10–11
Havdalah fun, 9
lulav shake, the real-deal, 29
music
  classroom-friendly guide to, 129–46
  for teens, 142–46
  Israeli, 141–42
  klezmer, 142–46

Yiddish, 140–141
nature
    fruits and vegetables, pick-'em-yourself, 83–84
    scouting, 124–25
operation feather-and-candle, 63–64
secular holidays, celebrating in a Jewish way, 93–98
seder
    Passover, 67–72
    Rosh Hashanah, Sephardic/Persian traditions, 18–20
    Tu B'Shvat, 46–48
sports
    Ga-Ga, 125–26
    Maccabi Games, 123–24

sukkah-building basics, 22
tashlich, 15–16
videos
    Israel, 175
    making your own, 181–82
    Shabbat and holidays, 173–75
    songs and stories, 176–79
volunteering, 101–7
    grassroots, 103
    homes and shelters, trips to, 105–6
    Memorial Day, 94
    mishloach manot, 61
    retirement home, showtime at, 104–5
    Thanksgiving, 97–98
    viva *Lag* difference, 81

By Craft

besamim box, make your own, 10
books, make your own, 170–71
candlesticks, can-do, 4–5
centerpiece, *sukkah*-in-a-*sukkah*, 27–28
"this challah's-for-the-birds" feeder, 126–27
crowns fit for a king or queen, 55–56
envelopes, make your own, 121–22
face paints, "Purim Punim," 55
family tree, how to grow a, 113–14
glow-in-the-dark Stars of David, 111
grogger, the "shake-rattle-and-roll," 54
Haman hat, 57
"Jew"elry, 78
Jewish calendar, designing your own, 21–23
Kiddush cup, "kid-ish," 5–6
matzah, undercover, 64–65

menorah making, miraculous, 36–37
mezuzah magic, 109–10
New Year's cards, sending the very best, 20–21
paper-cutting, prize-winning, 86–87
paper, turning back into a tree, 50–51
papier-mâché puppets, 58–59
place mats, playful, 112
seder, charting the course, 68
shofar, tooting your own, 14–15
Simchah strut, fun flags for, 33
tablecloth, the "super-appealing, spill-concealing," 8–9
tallit "tie-dye-enu," 114–17
Torah scrolls, tiny totin', 32
Tu B'Av cards, 90–91
tzedakah box, make your own, 102–3
videos, make your own, 181–82
wrapping paper, that's a wrap, 120–21

By Recipe

applesauce, appetizing, 40–41
candied apple, inside-out, 16–17
candy clay, all-purpose, 117–18
challah, Danielle's dough-licious, 6–8
charoset, Farid's persian version, 66–67
charoset, traditional Ashkenazi, 66
cheese blintzes, 84–85
cookies, "me-shugga," 119–20
falafel, the "stuff-it-'til-it-stuffs-you," 74–76

Hamantaschen, "so-good-you'll-eat-your-hat," 59–61
hummus, Aliza's spreadable edible incredible, 76–77
Israeli salad, slice 'n' dice, 77
latkes, lip-licking, 39–40
lulav "shake," the wacky 'n' tasty, 30
nut 'n' honey treats, old country, 17–18
soofganiyot, fry 'em and try 'em, 41–43

Bar/Bat Mitzvah

The Bar/Bat Mitzvah Memory Book
An Album for Treasuring the Spiritual Celebration
By Rabbi Jeffrey K. Salkin and Nina Salkin
A unique album for preserving the spiritual memories of the day, and for recording plans for the Jewish future ahead. Contents include space for creating or recording family history; teachings received from rabbi, cantor, and others; mitzvot and *tzedakot* chosen and carried out, etc.
8 x 10, 48 pp, Deluxe Hardcover, 2-color text, ribbon marker, ISBN 1-58023-111-X **$19.95**

Bar/Bat Mitzvah Basics: A Practical Family Guide to Coming of Age Together
Edited by Helen Leneman. Foreword by Rabbi Jeffrey K. Salkin.
6 x 9, 240 pp, Quality PB, ISBN 1-58023-151-9 **$18.95**

For Kids—Putting God on Your Guest List: How to Claim the Spiritual Meaning
of Your Bar or Bat Mitzvah *By Rabbi Jeffrey K. Salkin*
6 x 9, 144 pp, Quality PB, ISBN 1-58023-015-6 **$14.95** *For ages 11–12*

Putting God on the Guest List: How to Reclaim the Spiritual Meaning of Your
Child's Bar or Bat Mitzvah *By Rabbi Jeffrey K. Salkin*
6 x 9, 224 pp, Quality PB, ISBN 1-879045-59-1 **$16.95**

Tough Questions Jews Ask: A Young Adult's Guide to Building a Jewish Life
By Rabbi Edward Feinstein 6 x 9, 160 pp, Quality PB, ISBN 1-58023-139-X **$14.95** *For ages 13 & up*
Also Available: **Tough Questions Jews Ask Teacher's Guide**
8½ x 11, 72 pp, PB, ISBN 1-58023-187-X **$8.95**

Bible Study/Midrash

Hineini in Our Lives: Learning How to Respond to Others through 14 Biblical Texts,
and Personal Stories *By Norman J. Cohen*
6 x 9, 240 pp, Hardcover, ISBN 1-58023-131-4 **$23.95**

Ancient Secrets: Using the Stories of the Bible to Improve Our Everyday Lives
By Rabbi Levi Meier, Ph.D. 5½ x 8½, 288 pp, Quality PB, ISBN 1-58023-064-4 **$16.95**

Moses—The Prince, the Prophet: His Life, Legend & Message for Our Lives
By Rabbi Levi Meier, Ph.D.
6 x 9, 224 pp, Quality PB, ISBN 1-58023-069-5 **$16.95**

Self, Struggle & Change: Family Conflict Stories in Genesis and Their Healing Insights
for Our Lives *By Norman J. Cohen* 6 x 9, 224 pp, Quality PB, ISBN 1-879045-66-4 **$16.95**

Voices from Genesis: Guiding Us through the Stages of Life *By Norman J. Cohen*
6 x 9, 192 pp, Quality PB, ISBN 1-58023-118-7 **$16.95**

Congregation Resources

Becoming a Congregation of Learners: Learning as a Key to Revitalizing
Congregational Life *By Isa Aron, Ph.D. Foreword by Rabbi Lawrence A. Hoffman.*
6 x 9, 304 pp, Quality PB, ISBN 1-58023-089-X **$19.95**

Finding a Spiritual Home: How a New Generation of Jews Can Transform the
American Synagogue *By Rabbi Sidney Schwarz*
6 x 9, 352 pp, Quality PB, ISBN 1-58023-185-3 **$19.95**

Jewish Pastoral Care: A Practical Handbook from Traditional & Contemporary Sources
Edited by Rabbi Dayle A. Friedman 6 x 9, 464 pp, Hardcover, ISBN 1-58023-078-4 **$35.00**

The Self-Renewing Congregation: Organizational Strategies for Revitalizing
Congregational Life *By Isa Aron, Ph.D. Foreword by Dr. Ron Wolfson.*
6 x 9, 304 pp, Quality PB, ISBN 1-58023-166-7 **$19.95**

Or phone, fax, mail or e-mail to: **JEWISH LIGHTS Publishing**
Sunset Farm Offices, Route 4 • P.O. Box 237 • Woodstock, Vermont 05091
Tel: (802) 457-4000 • Fax: (802) 457-4004 • www.jewishlights.com
Credit card orders: **(800) 962-4544** (8:30AM–5:30PM ET Monday–Friday)
Generous discounts on quantity orders. SATISFACTION GUARANTEED. Prices subject to change.

Children's Books

What You Will See Inside a Synagogue
By Rabbi Lawrence A. Hoffman and Dr. Ron Wolfson; Full-color photos by Bill Aron
A colorful, fun-to-read introduction that explains the ways and whys of Jewish worship and religious life. Full-page photos; concise but informative descriptions of the objects used, the clergy and laypeople who have specific roles, and much more.
8½ x 10½, 32 pp, Full-color photos, Hardcover, ISBN 1-59473-012-1 **$17.99** *(A SkyLight Paths book)*

Because Nothing Looks Like God
By Lawrence and Karen Kushner
What is God like? Introduces children to the possibilities of spiritual life. Real-life examples of happiness and sadness invite us to explore, together with our children, the questions we all have about God.
11 x 8½, 32 pp, Full-color illus., Hardcover, ISBN 1-58023-092-X **$16.95** *For ages 4 & up*

Also Available: **Because Nothing Looks Like God Teacher's Guide**
8½ x 11, 22 pp, PB, ISBN 1-58023-140-3 **$6.95** *For ages 5–8*

Board Book Companions to *Because Nothing Looks Like God*
5 x 5, 24 pp, Full-color illus., SkyLight Paths Board Books, **$7.95** each *For ages 0–4*

What Does God Look Like? ISBN 1-893361-23-3

How Does God Make Things Happen? ISBN 1-893361-24-1

Where Is God? ISBN 1-893361-17-9

The 11th Commandment: Wisdom from Our Children
by The Children of America
"If there were an Eleventh Commandment, what would it be?" Children of many religious denominations across America answer in their own drawings and words.
8 x 10, 48 pp, Full-color illus., Hardcover, ISBN 1-879045-46-X **$16.95** *For all ages*

Jerusalem of Gold: Jewish Stories of the Enchanted City
Retold by Howard Schwartz. Full-color illus. by Neil Waldman.
A beautiful and engaging collection of historical and legendary stories for children. Based on Talmud, midrash, Jewish folklore, and mystical and Hasidic sources.
8 x 10, 64 pp, Full-color illus., Hardcover, ISBN 1-58023-149-7 **$18.95** *For ages 7 & up*

The Book of Miracles: A Young Person's Guide to Jewish Spiritual Awareness
By Lawrence Kushner. All-new illustrations by the author.
6 x 9, 96 pp, 2-color illus., Hardcover, ISBN 1-879045-78-8 **$16.95** *For ages 9–13*

In Our Image: God's First Creatures
By Nancy Sohn Swartz
9 x 12, 32 pp, Full-color illus., Hardcover, ISBN 1-879045-99-0 **$16.95** *For ages 4 & up*

Also Available as a Board Book: **How Did the Animals Help God?**
5 x 5, 24 pp, Board, Full-color illus., ISBN 1-59473-044-X **$7.99** *For ages 0–4 (A SkyLight Paths book)*

From SKYLIGHT PATHS PUBLISHING

Becoming Me: A Story of Creation
By Martin Boroson. Full-color illus. by Christopher Gilvan-Cartwright.
Told in the personal "voice" of the Creator, a story about creation and relationship that is about each one of us.
8 x 10, 32 pp, Full-color illus., Hardcover, ISBN 1-893361-11-X **$16.95** *For ages 4 & up*

Ten Amazing People: And How They Changed the World
By Maura D. Shaw. Foreword by Dr. Robert Coles. Full-color illus. by Stephen Marchesi.
Black Elk • Dorothy Day • Malcolm X • Mahatma Gandhi • Martin Luther King, Jr. • Mother Teresa • Janusz Korczak • Desmond Tutu • Thich Nhat Hanh • Albert Schweitzer.
8½ x 11, 48 pp, Full-color illus., Hardcover, ISBN 1-893361-47-0 **$17.95** *For ages 7 & up*

Where Does God Live? *By August Gold and Matthew J. Perlman*
Helps young readers develop a personal understanding of God.
10 x 8½, 32 pp, Full-color photo illus., Quality PB, ISBN 1-893361-39-X **$8.99** *For ages 3–6*

Children's Books
by Sandy Eisenberg Sasso

Adam & Eve's First Sunset: God's New Day
Engaging new story explores fear and hope, faith and gratitude in ways that will delight kids and adults—inspiring us to bless each of God's days and nights.
9 x 12, 32 pp, Full-color illus., Hardcover, ISBN 1-58023-177-2 **$17.95** *For ages 4 & up*

But God Remembered
Stories of Women from Creation to the Promised Land
Four different stories of women—Lillith, Serach, Bityah, and the Daughters of Z—teach us important values through their faith and actions.
9 x 12, 32 pp, Full-color illus., Hardcover, ISBN 1-879045-43-5 **$16.95** *For ages 8 & up*

Cain & Abel: Finding the Fruits of Peace
Shows children that we have the power to deal with anger in positive ways. Provides questions for kids and adults to explore together.
9 x 12, 32 pp, Full-color illus., Hardcover, ISBN 1-58023-123-3 **$16.95** *For ages 5 & up*

God in Between
If you wanted to find God, where would you look? This magical, mythical tale teaches that God can be found where we are: within all of us and the relationships between us.
9 x 12, 32 pp, Full-color illus., Hardcover, ISBN 1-879045-86-9 **$16.95** *For ages 4 & up*

God's Paintbrush: Special 10th Anniversary Edition
Wonderfully interactive, invites children of all faiths and backgrounds to encounter God through moments in their own lives. Provides questions adult and child can explore together.
11 x 8½, 32 pp, Full-color illus., Hardcover, ISBN 1-58023-195-0 **$17.95** *For ages 4 & up*

Also Available: **God's Paintbrush Teacher's Guide**
8½ x 11, 32 pp, PB, ISBN 1-879045-57-5 **$8.95**

God's Paintbrush Celebration Kit
A Spiritual Activity Kit for Teachers and Students of All Faiths, All Backgrounds
Additional activity sheets available:
8-Student Activity Sheet Pack (40 sheets/5 sessions), ISBN 1-58023-058-X **$19.95**
Single-Student Activity Sheet Pack (5 sessions), ISBN 1-58023-059-8 **$3.95**

In God's Name
Like an ancient myth in its poetic text and vibrant illustrations, this award-winning modern fable about the search for God's name celebrates the diversity and, at the same time, the unity of all people.
9 x 12, 32 pp, Full-color illus., Hardcover, ISBN 1-879045-26-5 **$16.99** *For ages 4 & up*

Also Available as a Board Book: **What Is God's Name?**
5 x 5, 24 pp, Board, Full-color illus., ISBN 1-893361-10-1 **$7.99** *For ages 0–4 (A SkyLight Paths book)*

Also Available: **In God's Name video and study guide**
Computer animation, original music, and children's voices. 18 min. **$29.99**

Also Available in Spanish: **El nombre de Dios**
9 x 12, 32 pp, Full-color illus., Hardcover, ISBN 1-893361-63-2 **$16.95** *(A SkyLight Paths book)*

Noah's Wife: The Story of Naamah
When God tells Noah to bring the animals of the world onto the ark, God also calls on Naamah, Noah's wife, to save each plant on Earth. Based on an ancient text.
9 x 12, 32 pp, Full-color illus., Hardcover, ISBN 1-58023-134-9 **$16.95** *For ages 4 & up*

Also Available as a Board Book: **Naamah, Noah's Wife**
5 x 5, 24 pp, Full-color illus., Board, ISBN 1-893361-56-X **$7.95** *For ages 0–4 (A SkyLight Paths book)*

For Heaven's Sake: Finding God in Unexpected Places
9 x 12, 32 pp, Full-color illus., Hardcover, ISBN 1-58023-054-7 **$16.95** *For ages 4 & up*

God Said Amen: Finding the Answers to Our Prayers
9 x 12, 32 pp, Full-color illus., Hardcover, ISBN 1-58023-080-6 **$16.95** *For ages 4 & up*

Current Events/History

The Story of the Jews: A 4,000-Year Adventure—A Graphic History Book
Written & illustrated by Stan Mack
Through witty, illustrated narrative, we visit all the major happenings from biblical times to the twenty-first century. Celebrates the major characters and events that have shaped the Jewish people and culture.
6 x 9, 288 pp, illus., Quality PB, ISBN 1-58023-155-1 **$16.95**

The Jewish Prophet: Visionary Words from Moses and Miriam to Henrietta Szold and A. J. Heschel   *By Rabbi Michael J. Shire*
6½ x 8½, 128 pp, 123 full-color illus., Hardcover, ISBN 1-58023-168-3 **$25.00**

Shared Dreams: Martin Luther King, Jr. & the Jewish Community
By Rabbi Marc Schneier. Preface by Martin Luther King III.
6 x 9, 240 pp, Hardcover, ISBN 1-58023-062-8 **$24.95**

"Who Is a Jew?": Conversations, Not Conclusions   *By Meryl Hyman*
6 x 9, 272 pp, Quality PB, ISBN 1-58023-052-0 **$16.95**

Ecology

Ecology & the Jewish Spirit: Where Nature & the Sacred Meet
Edited by Ellen Bernstein   6 x 9, 288 pp, Quality PB, ISBN 1-58023-082-2 **$16.95**

Torah of the Earth: Exploring 4,000 Years of Ecology in Jewish Thought
Vol. 1: Biblical Israel: One Land, One People; Rabbinic Judaism: One People, Many Lands
Vol. 2: Zionism: One Land, Two Peoples; Eco-Judaism: One Earth, Many Peoples
Edited by Rabbi Arthur Waskow
Vol. 1: 6 x 9, 272 pp, Quality PB, ISBN 1-58023-086-5 **$19.95**
Vol. 2: 6 x 9, 336 pp, Quality PB, ISBN 1-58023-087-3 **$19.95**

Grief/Healing

Against the Dying of the Light: A Parent's Story of Love, Loss and Hope
By Leonard Fein
In this unusual exploration of heartbreak and healing, Leonard Fein chronicles the sudden death of his 30-year-old daughter and shares the hard-earned wisdom that emerges in the face of loss and grief.
5½ x 8½, 176 pp, Quality PB, ISBN 1-58023-197-7 **$15.99**

Grief in Our Seasons: A Mourner's Kaddish Companion   *By Rabbi Kerry M. Olitzky*
4½ x 6½, 448 pp, Quality PB, ISBN 1-879045-55-9 **$15.95**

Healing of Soul, Healing of Body: Spiritual Leaders Unfold the Strength & Solace in Psalms   *Edited by Rabbi Simkha Y. Weintraub, C.S.W.*
6 x 9, 128 pp, 2-color illus. text, Quality PB, ISBN 1-879045-31-1 **$14.95**

Jewish Paths toward Healing and Wholeness: A Personal Guide to Dealing with Suffering   *By Rabbi Kerry M. Olitzky. Foreword by Debbie Friedman.*
6 x 9, 192 pp, Quality PB, ISBN 1-58023-068-7 **$15.95**

Mourning & Mitzvah, 2nd Edition: A Guided Journal for Walking the Mourner's Path through Grief to Healing   *By Anne Brener, L.C.S.W.*
7½ x 9, 304 pp, Quality PB, ISBN 1-58023-113-6 **$19.95**

The Perfect Stranger's Guide to Funerals and Grieving Practices
A Guide to Etiquette in Other People's Religious Ceremonies   *Edited by Stuart M. Matlins*
6 x 9, 240 pp, Quality PB, ISBN 1-893361-20-9 **$16.95**   *(A SkyLight Paths book)*

Tears of Sorrow, Seeds of Hope: A Jewish Spiritual Companion for Infertility and Pregnancy Loss   *By Rabbi Nina Beth Cardin*
6 x 9, 192 pp, Hardcover, ISBN 1-58023-017-2 **$19.95**

A Time to Mourn, A Time to Comfort: A Guide to Jewish Bereavement and Comfort   *By Dr. Ron Wolfson*   7 x 9, 336 pp, Quality PB, ISBN 1-879045-96-6 **$18.95**

When a Grandparent Dies: A Kid's Own Remembering Workbook for Dealing with Shiva and the Year Beyond   *By Nechama Liss-Levinson, Ph.D.*
8 x 10, 48 pp, 2-color text, Hardcover, ISBN 1-879045-44-3 **$15.95**   *For ages 7–13*

Abraham Joshua Heschel

The Earth Is the Lord's: The Inner World of the Jew in Eastern Europe
5½ x 8, 128 pp, Quality PB, ISBN 1-879045-42-7 **$14.95**

Israel: An Echo of Eternity *New Introduction by Susannah Heschel*
5½ x 8, 272 pp, Quality PB, ISBN 1-879045-70-2 **$19.95**

A Passion for Truth: Despair and Hope in Hasidism
5½ x 8, 352 pp, Quality PB, ISBN 1-879045-41-9 **$18.99**

Holidays/Holy Days

Reclaiming Judaism as a Spiritual Practice: Holy Days and Shabbat
By Rabbi Goldie Milgram
Provides a framework for understanding the powerful and often unexplained
intellectual, emotional, and spiritual tools that are essential for a lively, relevant,
and fulfilling Jewish spiritual practice. 7 x 9, 272 pp, Quality PB, ISBN 1-58023-205-1 **$19.99**

7th Heaven: Celebrating Shabbat with Rebbe Nachman of Breslov
By Moshe Mykoff with the Breslov Research Institute
Based on the teachings of Rebbe Nachman of Breslov. Explores the art of con-
sciously observing Shabbat and understanding in-depth many of the day's traditional spiritual practices. 5⅛ x 8¼, 224 pp, Deluxe PB w/flaps, ISBN 1-58023-175-6 **$18.95**

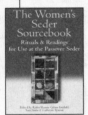

The Women's Passover Companion
Women's Reflections on the Festival of Freedom
Edited by Rabbi Sharon Cohen Anisfeld, Tara Mohr, and Catherine Spector
Groundbreaking. A provocative conversation about women's relationships to
Passover as well as the roots and meanings of women's seders.
6 x 9, 352 pp, Hardcover, ISBN 1-58023-128-4 **$24.95**

The Women's Seder Sourcebook
Rituals & Readings for Use at the Passover Seder
Edited by Rabbi Sharon Cohen Anisfeld, Tara Mohr, and Catherine Spector
Gathers the voices of more than one hundred women in readings, personal and
creative reflections, commentaries, blessings, and ritual suggestions that can be
incorporated into your Passover celebration as supplements to or substitutes for
traditional passages of the haggadah.
6 x 9, 384 pp, Hardcover, ISBN 1-58023-136-5 **$24.95**

Creating Lively Passover Seders: A Sourcebook of Engaging Tales, Texts & Activities
By David Arnow, Ph.D. 7 x 9, 416 pp, Quality PB, ISBN 1-58023-184-5 **$24.99**

Hanukkah, 2nd Edition: The Family Guide to Spiritual Celebration
By Dr. Ron Wolfson. Edited by Joel Lurie Grishaver.
7 x 9, 240 pp, illus., Quality PB, ISBN 1-58023-122-5 **$18.95**

The Jewish Family Fun Book: Holiday Projects, Everyday Activities, and Travel Ideas
with Jewish Themes *By Danielle Dardashti and Roni Sarig. Illus. by Avi Katz.*
6 x 9, 288 pp, 70+ b/w illus. & diagrams, Quality PB, ISBN 1-58023-171-3 **$18.95**

The Jewish Gardening Cookbook: Growing Plants & Cooking for
Holidays & Festivals *By Michael Brown* 6 x 9, 224 pp, 30+ illus., Quality PB, ISBN 1-58023-116-0 **$16.95**

The Jewish Lights Book of Fun Classroom Activities: Simple and Seasonal
Projects for Teachers and Students *By Danielle Dardashti and Roni Sarig*
6 x 9, 240 pp, Quality PB, ISBN 1-58023-206-X **$19.99**

Passover, 2nd Edition: The Family Guide to Spiritual Celebration
By Dr. Ron Wolfson with Joel Lurie Grishaver 7 x 9, 352 pp, Quality PB, ISBN 1-58023-174-8 **$19.95**

Shabbat, 2nd Edition: The Family Guide to Preparing for and Celebrating the Sabbath
By Dr. Ron Wolfson 7 x 9, 320 pp, illus., Quality PB, ISBN 1-58023-164-0 **$19.95**

Sharing Blessings: Children's Stories for Exploring the Spirit of the Jewish Holidays
By Rahel Musleah and Michael Klayman
8½ x 11, 64 pp, Full-color illus., Hardcover, ISBN 1-879045-71-0 **$18.95** *For ages 6 & up*

Inspiration

God in All Moments
Mystical & Practical Spiritual Wisdom from Hasidic Masters
Edited and translated by Or N. Rose with Ebn D. Leader
Hasidic teachings on how to be mindful in religious practice and cultivating every-day ethical behavior—*hanhagot.* 5½ x 8½, 192 pp, Quality PB, ISBN 1-58023-186-1 **$16.95**

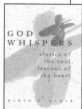

Our Dance with God: Finding Prayer, Perspective and Meaning in the Stories of Our Lives *By Karyn D. Kedar*
Inspiring spiritual insight to guide you on your life journeys and teach you to live and thrive in two conflicting worlds: the rational/material and the spiritual.
6 x 9, 176 pp, Quality PB, ISBN 1-58023-202-7 **$16.99**

Also Available: **The Dance of the Dolphin** (Hardcover edition of *Our Dance with God*)
6 x 9, 176 pp, Hardcover, ISBN 1-58023-154-3 **$19.95**

The Empty Chair: Finding Hope and Joy—Timeless Wisdom from a Hasidic Master, Rebbe Nachman of Breslov *Adapted by Moshe Mykoff and the Breslov Research Institute*
4 x 6, 128 pp, 2-color text, Deluxe PB w/flaps, ISBN 1-879045-67-2 **$9.95**

The Gentle Weapon: Prayers for Everyday and Not-So-Everyday Moments—Timeless Wisdom from the Teachings of the Hasidic Master, Rebbe Nachman of Breslov *Adapted by Moshe Mykoff and S. C. Mizrahi, together with the Breslov Research Institute*
4 x 6, 144 pp, 2-color text, Deluxe PB w/flaps, ISBN 1-58023-022-9 **$9.95**

God Whispers: Stories of the Soul, Lessons of the Heart *By Karyn D. Kedar*
6 x 9, 176 pp, Quality PB, ISBN 1-58023-088-1 **$15.95**

An Orphan in History: One Man's Triumphant Search for His Jewish Roots
By Paul Cowan. Afterword by Rachel Cowan. 6 x 9, 288 pp, Quality PB, ISBN 1-58023-135-7 **$16.95**

Restful Reflections: Nighttime Inspiration to Calm the Soul, Based on Jewish Wisdom
By Rabbi Kerry M. Olitzky & Rabbi Lori Forman 4½ x 6½, 448 pp, Quality PB, ISBN 1-58023-091-1 **$15.95**

Sacred Intentions: Daily Inspiration to Strengthen the Spirit, Based on Jewish Wisdom
By Rabbi Kerry M. Olitzky and Rabbi Lori Forman 4½ x 6½, 448 pp, Quality PB, ISBN 1-58023-061-X **$15.95**

Kabbalah/Mysticism/Enneagram

Seek My Face: A Jewish Mystical Theology
By Dr. Arthur Green
This classic work of contemporary Jewish theology, revised and updated, is a profound, deeply personal statement of the lasting truths of Jewish mysticism and the basic faith claims of Judaism. A tool for anyone seeking the elusive presence of God in the world. 6 x 9, 304 pp, Quality PB, ISBN 1-58023-130-6 **$19.95**

Zohar: Annotated & Explained
Translation and annotation by Dr. Daniel C. Matt. Foreword by Andrew Harvey
Offers insightful yet unobtrusive commentary to the masterpiece of Jewish mysticism that explains references and mystical symbols, shares wisdom of spiritual masters, and clarifies the *Zohar*'s bold claim: We have always been taught that we need God, but in order to manifest in the world, God needs us.
5½ x 8½, 160 pp, Quality PB, ISBN 1-893361-51-9 **$15.99** *(A SkyLight Paths book)*

Cast in God's Image: Discover Your Personality Type Using the Enneagram and Kabbalah
By Rabbi Howard A. Addison
7 x 9, 176 pp, Quality PB, Layflat binding, 20+ journaling exercises, ISBN 1-58023-124-1 **$16.95**

Ehyeh: A Kabbalah for Tomorrow *By Dr. Arthur Green*
6 x 9, 224 pp, Quality PB, ISBN 1-58023-213-2 **$16.99;** Hardcover, ISBN 1-58023-125-X **$21.99**

The Enneagram and Kabbalah: Reading Your Soul *By Rabbi Howard A. Addison*
6 x 9, 176 pp, Quality PB, ISBN 1-58023-001-6 **$15.95**

Finding Joy: A Practical Spiritual Guide to Happiness *By Dannel I. Schwartz with Mark Hass*
6 x 9, 192 pp, Quality PB, ISBN 1-58023-009-1 **$14.95;** Hardcover, ISBN 1-879045-53-2 **$19.95**

The Gift of Kabbalah: Discovering the Secrets of Heaven, Renewing Your Life on Earth
By Tamar Frankiel, Ph.D.
6 x 9, 256 pp, Quality PB, ISBN 1-58023-141-1 **$16.95;** Hardcover, ISBN 1-58023-108-X **$21.95**

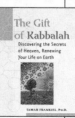

The Way Into Jewish Mystical Tradition *By Lawrence Kushner*
6 x 9, 224 pp, Quality PB, ISBN 1-58023-200-0 **$18.99;** Hardcover, ISBN 1-58023-029-6 **$21.95**

Life Cycle

Marriage / Parenting / Family / Aging

Jewish Fathers: A Legacy of Love
Photographs by Lloyd Wolf. Essays by Paula Wolfson. Foreword by Harold S. Kushner.
Honors the role of contemporary Jewish fathers in America. Each father tells in his own words what it means to be a parent and Jewish, and what he learned from his own father. Insightful photos. 9½ x 9⅞, 144 pp with 100+ duotone photos, Hardcover, ISBN 1-58023-204-3 **$30.00**

The New Jewish Baby Album: Creating and Celebrating the Beginning of a Spiritual Life—A Jewish Lights Companion
By the Editors at Jewish Lights. Foreword by Anita Diamant. Preface by Sandy Eisenberg Sasso.
A spiritual keepsake that will be treasured for generations. More than just a memory book, *shows you how—and why it's important*—to create a Jewish home and a Jewish life. 8 x 10, 64 pp, Deluxe Padded Hardcover, Full-color illus., ISBN 1-58023-138-1 **$19.95**

The Jewish Pregnancy Book: A Resource for the Soul, Body & Mind during Pregnancy, Birth & the First Three Months
By Sandy Falk, M.D., and Rabbi Daniel Judson, with Steven A. Rapp
Includes medical information on fetal development, pre-natal testing and more, from a liberal Jewish perspective; prenatal *Aleph-Bet* yoga; and prayers and rituals for each stage of pregnancy. 7 x 10, 208 pp, Quality PB, b/w illus., ISBN 1-58023-178-0 **$16.95**

Celebrating Your New Jewish Daughter: Creating Jewish Ways to Welcome Baby Girls into the Covenant—New and Traditional Ceremonies
By Debra Nussbaum Cohen 6 x 9, 272 pp, Quality PB, ISBN 1-58023-090-3 **$18.95**

The New Jewish Baby Book: Names, Ceremonies & Customs—A Guide for Today's Families *By Anita Diamant* 6 x 9, 336 pp, Quality PB, ISBN 1-879045-28-1 **$18.95**

Parenting As a Spiritual Journey: Deepening Ordinary and Extraordinary Events into Sacred Occasions *By Rabbi Nancy Fuchs-Kreimer* 6 x 9, 224 pp, Quality PB, ISBN 1-58023-016-4 **$16.95**

Embracing the Covenant: Converts to Judaism Talk About Why & How
Edited and with introductions by Rabbi Allan Berkowitz and Patti Moskovitz
6 x 9, 192 pp, Quality PB, ISBN 1-879045-50-8 **$16.95**

The Guide to Jewish Interfaith Family Life: An InterfaithFamily.com Handbook
Edited by Ronnie Friedland and Edmund Case 6 x 9, 384 pp, Quality PB, ISBN 1-58023-153-5 **$18.95**

Introducing My Faith and My Community
The Jewish Outreach Institute Guide for the Christian in a Jewish Interfaith Relationship
By Rabbi Kerry M. Olitzky 6 x 9, 176 pp, Quality PB, ISBN 1-58023-192-6 **$16.99**

Making a Successful Jewish Interfaith Marriage: The Jewish Outreach Institute Guide to Opportunities, Challenges and Resources
By Rabbi Kerry M. Olitzky with Joan Peterson Littman 6 x 9, 176 pp, Quality PB, ISBN 1-58023-170-5 **$16.95**

How to Be a Perfect Stranger, 3rd Edition: The Essential Religious Etiquette Handbook *Edited by Stuart M. Matlins and Arthur J. Magida*
The indispensable guide to the rituals and celebrations of the major religions and denominations in North America from the perspective of an interested guest of any other faith. 6 x 9, 432 pp, Quality PB, ISBN 1-893361-67-5 **$19.95** (A SkyLight Paths book)

The Creative Jewish Wedding Book: A Hands-On Guide to New & Old Traditions, Ceremonies & Celebrations *By Gabrielle Kaplan-Mayer*
Provides the tools to create the most meaningful Jewish traditional or alternative wedding by using ritual elements to express your unique style and spirituality. 9 x 9, 288 pp, b/w photos, Quality PB, ISBN 1-58023-194-2 **$19.99**

Divorce Is a Mitzvah: A Practical Guide to Finding Wholeness and Holiness When Your Marriage Dies *By Rabbi Perry Netter. Afterword by Rabbi Laura Geller.*
6 x 9, 224 pp, Quality PB, ISBN 1-58023-172-1 **$16.95**

A Heart of Wisdom: Making the Jewish Journey from Midlife through the Elder Years
Edited by Susan Berrin. Foreword by Harold Kushner. 6 x 9, 384 pp, Quality PB, ISBN 1-58023-051-2 **$18.95**

So That Your Values Live On: Ethical Wills and How to Prepare Them
Edited by Jack Riemer and Nathaniel Stampfer 6 x 9, 272 pp, Quality PB, ISBN 1-879045-34-6 **$18.95**

Meditation

The Handbook of Jewish Meditation Practices
A Guide for Enriching the Sabbath and Other Days of Your Life
By Rabbi David A. Cooper
Easy-to-learn meditation techniques for use on the Sabbath and every day, to help us return to the roots of traditional Jewish spirituality where Shabbat is a state of mind and soul. 6 x 9, 208 pp, Quality PB, ISBN 1-58023-102-0 **$16.95**

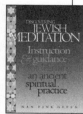

Discovering Jewish Meditation: Instruction & Guidance for Learning an Ancient Spiritual Practice *By Nan Fink Gefen, Ph.D.* 6 x 9, 208 pp, Quality PB, ISBN 1-58023-067-9 **$16.95**

A Heart of Stillness: A Complete Guide to Learning the Art of Meditation
By Rabbi David A. Cooper 5½ x 8½, 272 pp, Quality PB, ISBN 1-893361-03-9 **$16.95**
(A SkyLight Paths book)

Meditation from the Heart of Judaism: Today's Teachers Share Their Practices, Techniques, and Faith *Edited by Avram Davis*
6 x 9, 256 pp, Quality PB, ISBN 1-58023-049-0 **$16.95**

Silence, Simplicity & Solitude: A Complete Guide to Spiritual Retreat at Home
By Rabbi David A. Cooper 5½ x 8½, 336 pp, Quality PB, ISBN 1-893361-04-7 **$16.95**
(A SkyLight Paths book)

Three Gates to Meditation Practice: A Personal Journey into Sufism, Buddhism, and Judaism *By Rabbi David A. Cooper*
5½ x 8½, 240 pp, Quality PB, ISBN 1-893361-22-5 **$16.95** *(A SkyLight Paths book)*

The Way of Flame: A Guide to the Forgotten Mystical Tradition of Jewish Meditation
By Avram Davis 4½ x 8, 176 pp, Quality PB, ISBN 1-58023-060-1 **$15.95**

Ritual/Sacred Practice/Journaling

The Jewish Dream Book: The Key to Opening the Inner Meaning of Your Dreams *By Vanessa L. Ochs with Elizabeth Ochs; Full-color illus. by Kristina Swarner*
Instructions for how modern people can perform ancient Jewish dream practices and dream interpretations drawn from the Jewish wisdom tradition. For anyone who wants to understand their dreams—and themselves.
8 x 8, 120 pp, Full-color illus., Deluxe PB w/flaps, ISBN 1-58023-132-2 **$16.95**

The Jewish Journaling Book: How to Use Jewish Tradition to Write Your Life & Explore Your Soul *By Janet Ruth Falon*
Details the history of Jewish journaling throughout biblical and modern times, and teaches specific journaling techniques to help you create and maintain a vital journal, from a Jewish perspective. 8 x 8, 304 pp, Deluxe PB w/flaps, ISBN 1-58023-203-5 **$18.99**

The Rituals & Practices of a Jewish Life: A Handbook for Personal Spiritual Renewal *Edited by Rabbi Kerry M. Olitzky and Rabbi Daniel Judson*
6 x 9, 272 pp, illus., Quality PB, ISBN 1-58023-169-1 **$18.95**

The Book of Jewish Sacred Practices: CLAL's Guide to Everyday & Holiday Rituals & Blessings *Edited by Rabbi Irwin Kula and Vanessa L. Ochs, Ph.D.*
6 x 9, 368 pp, Quality PB, ISBN 1-58023-152-7 **$18.95**

Science Fiction/ Mystery & Detective Fiction

Mystery Midrash: An Anthology of Jewish Mystery & Detective Fiction
Edited by Lawrence W. Raphael. Preface by Joel Siegel.
6 x 9, 304 pp, Quality PB, ISBN 1-58023-055-5 **$16.95**

Criminal Kabbalah: An Intriguing Anthology of Jewish Mystery & Detective Fiction
Edited by Lawrence W. Raphael. Foreword by Laurie R. King.
6 x 9, 256 pp, Quality PB, ISBN 1-58023-109-8 **$16.95**

More Wandering Stars: An Anthology of Outstanding Stories of Jewish Fantasy and Science Fiction *Edited by Jack Dann. Introduction by Isaac Asimov.*
6 x 9, 192 pp, Quality PB, ISBN 1-58023-063-6 **$16.95**

Wandering Stars: An Anthology of Jewish Fantasy & Science Fiction
Edited by Jack Dann. Introduction by Isaac Asimov.
6 x 9, 272 pp, Quality PB, ISBN 1-58023-005-9 **$16.95**

Spirituality

The Alphabet of Paradise: An A–Z of Spirituality for Everyday Life
By Rabbi Howard Cooper
In twenty-six engaging chapters, Cooper spiritually illuminates the subjects of our daily lives—A to Z—examining these sources by using an ancient Jewish mystical method of interpretation that reveals both the literal and more allusive meanings of each. 5 x 7¾, 224 pp, Quality PB, ISBN 1-893361-80-2 **$16.95** *(A SkyLight Paths book)*

Does the Soul Survive?: A Jewish Journey to Belief in Afterlife, Past Lives & Living with Purpose *By Rabbi Elie Kaplan Spitz. Foreword by Brian L. Weiss, M.D.*
Spitz relates his own experiences and those shared with him by people he has worked with as a rabbi, and shows us that belief in afterlife and past lives, so often approached with reluctance, is in fact true to Jewish tradition.
6 x 9, 288 pp, Quality PB, ISBN 1-58023-165-9 **$16.95**; Hardcover, ISBN 1-58023-094-6 **$21.95**

First Steps to a New Jewish Spirit: Reb Zalman's Guide to Recapturing the Intimacy & Ecstasy in Your Relationship with God
By Rabbi Zalman M. Schachter-Shalomi with Donald Gropman
An extraordinary spiritual handbook that restores psychic and physical vigor by introducing us to new models and alternative ways of practicing Judaism. Offers meditation and contemplation exercises for enriching the most important aspects of everyday life. 6 x 9, 144 pp, Quality PB, ISBN 1-58023-182-9 **$16.95**

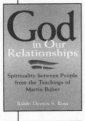

God in Our Relationships: Spirituality between People from the Teachings of Martin Buber *By Rabbi Dennis S. Ross*
On the eightieth anniversary of Buber's classic work, we can discover new answers to critical issues in our lives. Inspiring examples from Ross's own life—as congregational rabbi, father, hospital chaplain, social worker, and husband—illustrate Buber's difficult-to-understand ideas about how we encounter God and each other. 5½ x 8½, 160 pp, Quality PB, ISBN 1-58023-147-0 **$16.95**

The Jewish Lights Spirituality Handbook: A Guide to Understanding, Exploring & Living a Spiritual Life *Edited by Stuart M. Matlins*
What exactly is "Jewish" about spirituality? How do I make it a part of my life? Fifty of today's foremost spiritual leaders share their ideas and experience with us.
6 x 9, 456 pp, Quality PB, ISBN 1-58023-093-8 **$19.99**; Hardcover, ISBN 1-58023-100-4 **$24.95**

Bringing the Psalms to Life: How to Understand and Use the Book of Psalms
By Dr. Daniel F. Polish
6 x 9, 208 pp, Quality PB, ISBN 1-58023-157-8 **$16.95**; Hardcover, ISBN 1-58023-077-6 **$21.95**

God & the Big Bang: Discovering Harmony between Science & Spirituality
By Dr. Daniel C. Matt 6 x 9, 216 pp, Quality PB, ISBN 1-879045-89-3 **$16.95**

Godwrestling—Round 2: Ancient Wisdom, Future Paths
By Rabbi Arthur Waskow 6 x 9, 352 pp, Quality PB, ISBN 1-879045-72-9 **$18.95**

One God Clapping: The Spiritual Path of a Zen Rabbi *By Rabbi Alan Lew with Sherril Jaffe*
5½ x 8½, 336 pp, Quality PB, ISBN 1-58023-115-2 **$16.95**

The Path of Blessing: Experiencing the Energy and Abundance of the Divine
By Rabbi Marcia Prager 5½ x 8½, 240 pp, Quality PB, ISBN 1-58023-148-9 **$16.95**

Six Jewish Spiritual Paths: A Rationalist Looks at Spirituality *By Rabbi Rifat Sonsino*
6 x 9, 208 pp, Quality PB, ISBN 1-58023-167-5 **$16.95**; Hardcover, ISBN 1-58023-095-4 **$21.95**

Soul Judaism: Dancing with God into a New Era
By Rabbi Wayne Dosick 5½ x 8½, 304 pp, Quality PB, ISBN 1-58023-053-9 **$16.95**

Stepping Stones to Jewish Spiritual Living: Walking the Path Morning, Noon, and Night *By Rabbi James L. Mirel and Karen Bonnell Werth*
6 x 9, 240 pp, Quality PB, ISBN 1-58023-074-1 **$16.95**; Hardcover, ISBN 1-58023-003-2 **$21.95**

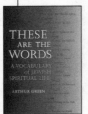

There Is No Messiah... and You're It: The Stunning Transformation of Judaism's Most Provocative Idea *By Rabbi Robert N. Levine, D.D.*
6 x 9, 192 pp, Hardcover, ISBN 1-58023-173-X **$21.95**

These Are the Words: A Vocabulary of Jewish Spiritual Life *By Dr. Arthur Green*
6 x 9, 304 pp, Quality PB, ISBN 1-58023-107-1 **$18.95**

Spirituality/Lawrence Kushner

The Book of Letters: A Mystical Hebrew Alphabet
Popular Hardcover Edition, 6 x 9, 80 pp, 2-color text, ISBN 1-879045-00-1 **$24.95**
Deluxe Gift Edition with slipcase, 9 x 12, 80 pp, 4-color text, Hardcover, ISBN 1-879045-01-X **$79.95**
Collector's Limited Edition, 9 x 12, 80 pp, gold foil embossed pages, w/limited edition silkscreened
print, ISBN 1-879045-04-4 **$349.00**

The Book of Miracles: A Young Person's Guide to Jewish Spiritual Awareness
All-new illustrations by the author
6 x 9, 96 pp, 2-color illus., Hardcover, ISBN 1-879045-78-8 **$16.95** *For ages 9–13*

The Book of Words: Talking Spiritual Life, Living Spiritual Talk
6 x 9, 160 pp, Quality PB, ISBN 1-58023-020-2 **$16.95**

Eyes Remade for Wonder: A Lawrence Kushner Reader
Introduction by Thomas Moore
6 x 9, 240 pp, Quality PB, ISBN 1-58023-042-3 **$18.95;** Hardcover, ISBN 1-58023-014-8 **$23.95**

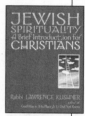

God Was in This Place & I, i Did Not Know
Finding Self, Spirituality and Ultimate Meaning
6 x 9, 192 pp, Quality PB, ISBN 1-879045-33-8 **$16.95**

Honey from the Rock: An Introduction to Jewish Mysticism
6 x 9, 176 pp, Quality PB, ISBN 1-58023-073-3 **$16.95**

Invisible Lines of Connection: Sacred Stories of the Ordinary
5½ x 8½, 160 pp, Quality PB, ISBN 1-879045-98-2 **$15.95**

Jewish Spirituality—A Brief Introduction for Christians
5½ x 8½, 112 pp, Quality PB Original, ISBN 1-58023-150-0 **$12.95**

The River of Light: Jewish Mystical Awareness
6 x 9, 192 pp, Quality PB, ISBN 1-58023-096-2 **$16.95**

The Way Into Jewish Mystical Tradition
6 x 9, 224 pp, Quality PB, ISBN 1-58023-200-0 **$18.99;** Hardcover, ISBN 1-58023-029-6 **$21.95**

Spirituality/Prayer

Pray Tell: A Hadassah Guide to Jewish Prayer
*By Rabbi Jules Harlow, with contributions from Tamara Cohen, Rochelle Furstenberg, Rabbi Daniel
Gordis, Leora Tanenbaum, and many others*
A guide to traditional Jewish prayer enriched with insight and wisdom from a
broad variety of viewpoints—from Orthodox, Conservative, Reform, and
Reconstructionist Judaism to New Age and feminist.
8½ x 11, 400 pp, Quality PB, ISBN 1-58023-163-2 **$29.95**

My People's Prayer Book Series
Traditional Prayers, Modern Commentaries
Edited by Rabbi Lawrence A. Hoffman
Provides diverse and exciting commentary to the traditional liturgy, helping modern
men and women find new wisdom in Jewish prayer, and bring liturgy into their lives.
Each book includes Hebrew text, modern translation, and commentaries from all
perspectives of the Jewish world.

Vol. 1—The *Sh'ma* and Its Blessings
7 x 10, 168 pp, Hardcover, ISBN 1-879045-79-6 **$23.95**
Vol. 2—The *Amidah*
7 x 10, 240 pp, Hardcover, ISBN 1-879045-80-X **$24.95**
Vol. 3—*P'sukei D'zimrah* (Morning Psalms)
7 x 10, 240 pp, Hardcover, ISBN 1-879045-81-8 **$24.95**
Vol. 4—*Seder K'riat Hatorah* (The Torah Service)
7 x 10, 264 pp, Hardcover, ISBN 1-879045-82-6 **$23.95**
Vol. 5—*Birkhot Hashachar* (Morning Blessings)
7 x 10, 240 pp, Hardcover, ISBN 1-879045-83-4 **$24.95**
Vol. 6—*Tachanun* and Concluding Prayers
7 x 10, 240 pp, Hardcover., ISBN 1-879045-84-2 **$24.95**
Vol. 7—Shabbat at Home
7 x 10, 240 pp, Hardcover, ISBN 1-879045-85-0 **$24.95**
Vol. 8—Shabbat in the Synagogue
7 x 10, 240 pp (est), Hardcover, ISBN 1-58023-121-7 **$24.99**

Spirituality/The Way Into... Series

The Way Into... Series offers an accessible and highly usable "guided tour" of the Jewish faith, people, history and beliefs—in total, an introduction to Judaism that will enable you to understand and interact with the sacred texts of the Jewish tradition. Each volume is written by a leading contemporary scholar and teacher, and explores one key aspect of Judaism. *The Way Into...* enables all readers to achieve a real sense of Jewish cultural literacy through guided study.

The Way Into Encountering God in Judaism *By Neil Gillman*
6 x 9, 240 pp, Quality PB, ISBN 1-58023-199-3 **$18.99**; Hardcover, ISBN 1-58023-025-3 **$21.95**

Also Available: **The Jewish Approach to God: A Brief Introduction for Christians**
By Neil Gillman 5½ x 8½, 192 pp, Quality PB, ISBN 1-58023-190-X **$16.95**

The Way Into Jewish Mystical Tradition *By Lawrence Kushner*
6 x 9, 224 pp, Quality PB, ISBN 1-58023-200-0 **$18.99**; Hardcover, ISBN 1-58023-029-6 **$21.95**

The Way Into Jewish Prayer *By Lawrence A. Hoffman*
6 x 9, 224 pp, Quality PB, ISBN 1-58023-201-9 **$18.99**; Hardcover, ISBN 1-58023-027-X **$21.95**

The Way Into Torah *By Norman J. Cohen*
6 x 9, 176 pp, Quality PB, ISBN 1-58023-198-5 **$16.99**; Hardcover, ISBN 1-58023-028-8 **$21.95**

Spirituality in the Workplace

Being God's Partner
How to Find the Hidden Link Between Spirituality and Your Work
By Rabbi Jeffrey K. Salkin. Introduction by Norman Lear.
6 x 9, 192 pp, Quality PB, ISBN 1-879045-65-6 **$17.95**

The Business Bible: 10 New Commandments for Bringing Spirituality & Ethical
Values into the Workplace *By Rabbi Wayne Dosick*
5½ x 8½, 208 pp, Quality PB, ISBN 1-58023-101-2 **$14.95**

Spirituality and Wellness

Aleph-Bet Yoga
Embodying the Hebrew Letters for Physical and Spiritual Well-Being
By Steven A. Rapp. Foreword by Tamar Frankiel, Ph.D., and Judy Greenfeld. Preface by Hart Lazer
7 x 10, 128 pp, b/w photos, Quality PB, Layflat binding, ISBN 1-58023-162-4 **$16.95**

Entering the Temple of Dreams
Jewish Prayers, Movements, and Meditations for the End of the Day
By Tamar Frankiel, Ph.D., and Judy Greenfeld
7 x 10, 192 pp, illus., Quality PB, ISBN 1-58023-079-2 **$16.95**

Jewish Paths toward Healing and Wholeness: A Personal Guide to Dealing
with Suffering *By Rabbi Kerry M. Olitzky. Foreword by Debbie Friedman.*
6 x 9, 192 pp, Quality PB, ISBN 1-58023-068-7 **$15.95**

Minding the Temple of the Soul
Balancing Body, Mind, and Spirit through Traditional Jewish Prayer, Movement, and
Meditation *By Tamar Frankiel, Ph.D., and Judy Greenfeld*
7 x 10, 184 pp, illus., Quality PB, ISBN 1-879045-64-8 **$16.95**
Audiotape of the Blessings and Meditations: 60 min. **$9.95**
Videotape of the Movements and Meditations: 46 min. **$20.00**

Spirituality/Women's Interest

The Quotable Jewish Woman: Wisdom, Inspiration & Humor from the Mind & Heart *Edited and compiled by Elaine Bernstein Partnow*
The definitive collection of ideas, reflections, humor, and wit of over 300 Jewish women.
6 x 9, 496 pp, Hardcover, ISBN 1-58023-193-4 **$29.99**

Lifecycles, Vol. 1: Jewish Women on Life Passages & Personal Milestones
Edited and with introductions by Rabbi Debra Orenstein 6 x 9, 480 pp, Quality PB, ISBN 1-58023-018-0 **$19.95**

Lifecycles, Vol. 2: Jewish Women on Biblical Themes in Contemporary Life
Edited and with introductions by Rabbi Debra Orenstein and Rabbi Jane Rachel Litman
6 x 9, 464 pp, Quality PB, ISBN 1-58023-019-9 **$19.95**

Moonbeams: A Hadassah Rosh Hodesh Guide *Edited by Carol Diament, Ph.D.*
8½ x 11, 240 pp, Quality PB, ISBN 1-58023-099-7 **$20.00**

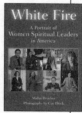

ReVisions: Seeing Torah through a Feminist Lens *By Rabbi Elyse Goldstein*
5½ x 8½, 224 pp, Quality PB, ISBN 1-58023-117-9 **$16.95**

White Fire: A Portrait of Women Spiritual Leaders in America
By Rabbi Malka Drucker. Photographs by Gay Block.
7 x 10, 320 pp, 30+ b/w photos, Hardcover, ISBN 1-893361-64-0 **$24.95** *(A SkyLight Paths book)*

Women of the Wall: Claiming Sacred Ground at Judaism's Holy Site
Edited by Phyllis Chesler and Rivka Haut 6 x 9, 496 pp, b/w photos, Hardcover, ISBN 1-58023-161-6 **$34.95**

The Women's Haftarah Commentary: New Insights from Women Rabbis on the 54 Weekly Haftarah Portions, the 5 Megillot & Special Shabbatot
Edited by Rabbi Elyse Goldstein 6 x 9, 560 pp, Hardcover, ISBN 1-58023-133-0 **$39.99**

The Women's Torah Commentary: New Insights from Women Rabbis on the 54 Weekly Torah Portions *Edited by Rabbi Elyse Goldstein*
6 x 9, 496 pp, Hardcover, ISBN 1-58023-076-8 **$34.95**

The Year Mom Got Religion: One Woman's Midlife Journey into Judaism
By Lee Meyerhoff Hendler 6 x 9, 208 pp, Quality PB, ISBN 1-58023-070-9 **$15.95**

See Holidays for *The Women's Passover Companion: Women's Reflections on the Festival of Freedom* and *The Women's Seder Sourcebook: Rituals & Readings for Use at the Passover Seder.*

Travel

Israel—A Spiritual Travel Guide: A Companion for the Modern Jewish Pilgrim
By Rabbi Lawrence A. Hoffman 4¾ x 10, 256 pp, Quality PB, illus., ISBN 1-879045-56-7 **$18.95**
Also Available: **The Israel Mission Leader's Guide** ISBN 1-58023-085-7 **$4.95**

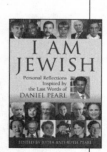

I Am Jewish
Personal Reflections Inspired by the Last Words of Daniel Pearl
Almost 150 Jews—both famous and not—from all walks of life, from all around the world, write about Identity, Heritage, Covenant / Chosenness and Faith, Humanity and Ethnicity, and *Tikkun Olam* and Justice.

Edited by Judea and Ruth Pearl
6 x 9, 304 pp, Hardcover, ISBN 1-58023-183-7 **$24.99**
Download a free copy of the *I Am Jewish Teacher's Guide* at our website: www.jewishlights.com

About Jewish Lights

People of all faiths and backgrounds yearn for books that attract, engage, educate, and spiritually inspire.

Our principal goal is to stimulate thought and help all people learn about who the Jewish People are, where they come from, and what the future can be made to hold. While people of our diverse Jewish heritage are the primary audience, our books speak to people in the Christian world as well and will broaden their understanding of Judaism and the roots of their own faith.

We bring to you authors who are at the forefront of spiritual thought and experience. While each has something different to say, they all say it in a voice that you can hear.

Our books are designed to welcome you and then to engage, stimulate, and inspire. We judge our success not only by whether or not our books are beautiful and commercially successful, but by whether or not they make a difference in your life.

For your information and convenience, at the back of this book we have provided a list of other Jewish Lights books you might find interesting and useful. They cover all the categories of your life:

Bar/Bat Mitzvah	Life Cycle
Bible Study / Midrash	Meditation
Children's Books	Parenting
Congregation Resources	Prayer
Current Events / History	Ritual / Sacred Practice
Ecology	Spirituality
Fiction: Mystery, Science Fiction	Theology / Philosophy
Grief / Healing	Travel
Holidays / Holy Days	Twelve Steps
Inspiration	Women's Interest
Kabbalah / Mysticism / Enneagram	

Stuart M. Matlins, Publisher